D0952574

JOHN GARDNER

A Study of the Short Fiction

Twayne's Studies in Short Fiction

Gordon Weaver, General Editor
Oklahoma State University

Photograph Courtesy of Joel Gardner

JOHN GARDNER

A Study of the Short Fiction

Jeff Henderson
University of Central Arkansas

TWAYNE PUBLISHERS • *BOSTON*
A Division of G. K. Hall & Co.

Twayne's Studies in Short Fiction Series, no. 15

Copyediting supervised by Barbara Sutton.
Book design and production by Gabrielle B. McDonald
Typeset in 10/12 Caslon by Compset, Inc.

First published 1990.
10 9 8 7 6 5 4 3 2 1

The paper used in this publication meets the minimum requirements of
American National Standard for Information Sciences—Permanence of Paper
for Printed Library Materials, ANSI Z39.48-1984. ∞™

Printed and bound in the United States of America.

Library of Congress Cataloging-in-Publication Data

Henderson, Jeff, 1943–
    John Gardner : a study of the short fiction / Jeff Henderson.
        p.   cm. — (Twayne's studies in short fiction ; no. 15)
    Includes bibliographical references (p.
    ISBN 0-8057-8326-1 (alk. paper)
    1. Gardner, John, 1933–   —Criticism and interpretation.
2. Short story.   I. Title.   II. Series.
PS3557.A712Z68   1990
813'.54—dc20   90-4114
                                                      CIP

Contents

Preface

John Gardner was a writer in a remarkably broad sense. He was also a teacher, scholar, critic, editor, musician, translator, and many other things. But more than all these—subsuming all these—he was a writer. Like many who devote their lives to the art and craft of writing, he started young, writing doggerel verse at age eight, he says in the posthumously published *On Becoming a Novelist*, and continuing through high school and college to write poems, stories, novels, and plays. Gardner's first important publication was a textbook anthology of thirty short stories and novellas entitled *The Forms of Fiction* (1962), which he edited in collaboration with Lennis Dunlap, an English department colleague at Chico State College (now California State University at Chico). Gardner and Dunlap supplied extensive critical commentary, analysis, and interpretation for many of the stories, including perhaps most significantly a substantial essay on "The Modern Writer's Use of the Sketch, Fable, Yarn, and Tale." From the beginning of his career Gardner was interested in the varieties of fiction.

Gardner's public career as a writer lasted for a scant twenty years, until his death at age forty-nine in a motorcycle accident on 14 September 1982. In that relatively brief span he published more than thirty books, including novels, poems, plays, translations, books of literary scholarship and criticism, librettos, children's books, and two collections of short fiction, *The King's Indian: Stories and Tales* (1974) and *The Art of Living and Other Stories* (1981), as well as numerous articles, essays, reviews, letters, various contributions to books (introductions, forewords, afterwords, etc.), and well over one hundred interviews. It was a literary career remarkable for both productivity and variety. Yet through it all there runs the constant thread of Gardner's interest in the art of fiction. Gardner ultimately became an artist and teacher of fiction, to the gradual exclusion of his production of other forms of writing and of his engagement in other areas of teaching. He spent the last several years of his life writing fiction and teaching the writing of fiction as director of the creative writing program at the State University of New York at Binghamton.

While Gardner's fame and reputation derive primarily from his novels, the fact is that he was vitally interested in all the forms of fiction: ancient and modern; long, short, and in-between; poetic forms as well as prose; dramatic as well as narrative. It is as if—and indeed I believe this to be the case—Gardner deliberately followed the example of Chaucer in the *Canterbury Tales* in seeking to write something in virtually every fictive genre and subgenre available to him as an author. Thus he wrote and published, in addition to his ten novels (including the posthumously published *Stillness* and *Shadows* [1986]), the epic poem *Jason and Medeia* (1973), a number of shorter poems, several opera librettos and radio plays, and some forty-one pieces of short fiction—short stories, novellas, and what Gardner classified as tales, or short fictions in which the usual conventions of the short story subgenre do not apply.

Although this book concerns specifically Gardner's work in short prose fiction, it must be noted that his short fiction in several important ways is of a piece with the longer works. One of the most striking features of Gardner's fiction generally is the coherence and consistency of the author's vision, the constancy of his recurring themes and messages. In these respects the short stories, the novels, and the epic poem constitute a virtual unity, in spite of their apparent diversity of form, style, setting, and character. It is one measure of Gardner's achievement as an artist that his various works are able to maintain their variety, that they do not strike the reader as mere repetitions and reworkings of the same themes and ideas.

The reasons for this sense of unity in apparent diversity are not far to seek. Generally, this is an effect all successful art achieves, more or less. Few things if any are new under the sun, in art as in life, and the successful artist is he who represents and recycles old materials in fresh and pleasing ways. In Gardner's case it is also true that he was dead serious about the writing of fiction; he believed, and frequently said, that it is the purpose and function of art (fiction) to clarify and improve life. His fiction therefore seeks to discover and inculcate values and beliefs that serve those ends, not didactically (he abhorred didactic fiction) but inductively, by dramatizing in plot and character the processes that lead to discovery. The result is that Gardner's themes recur insistently in his fiction, in a myriad of guises, arrived at by many different routes, but always affirming the values that Gardner had discovered—in the process of writing, he would insist—he could affirm.

Those themes include, most prominently, the centrality and efficacy of love and art, the value of human community and communion, the notions that life imitates art in ways more profound than ordinarily supposed and that in order to live successfully one should strive to "make life art," the universal tension between order and disorder, and the human potential for achieving what Gardner called mundane salvation.

The pages that follow offer, in part 1, an analysis of and commentary on Gardner's short fiction. The primary focus is on the stories and tales contained in the two collections previously mentioned, *The King's Indian* and *The Art of Living*, and the posthumously published "Julius Caesar and the Werewolf" (1984). Gardner's stories for children, published in collections entitled *Dragon, Dragon and Other Tales* (1975), *Gudgekin the Thistle Girl and Other Tales* (1976), and *The King of the Hummingbirds and Other Tales* (1977), are discussed less extensively but are shown to embody the same themes and concerns as his "adult" fiction. Part 2 presents a selection of Gardner's own comments on his fiction, and the art of fiction generally, drawn from published interviews and other sources. Part 3 offers a selection of the best previously published critical responses to Gardner's short fiction. The Chronology identifies significant dates in Gardner's life, mainly those which reflect the publishing history of his works and those which might be supposed to have had an important impact on his fiction. The Bibliography provides a comprehensive list of Gardner's short fiction publications in periodicals and collections, and a selected list of critical books, articles, interviews, and reviews dealing with Gardner's works.

My thanks are due to more people than I can name, for assistances too numerous and too various to chronicle. But I cannot fail to acknowledge the help, both witting and unwitting, I have received from other scholars and critics who have addressed their more considerable talents to Gardner's works. For facts, opinions, insights, and interpretations without which my own efforts would have been impossible, I am indebted to Leonard C. Butts, David Cowart, John M. Howell, Robert A. Morace, Gregory L. Morris, and others, whose writings constitute the best work that has been done on Gardner's fiction. I also wish to thank Peter Dzwonkoski, head of the Department of Rare Books and Special Collections at the University of Rochester, for acquiring and maintaining the Gardner Collection there, and for his gracious assistance in facilitating my use of those materials. I must also thank my department chairman, Phillip Anderson, and my dean, James

Dombek, for providing me with generous blocks of released time in which to complete this project, as well as the Research Council of the University of Central Arkansas for providing a travel grant that subsidized essential research. Finally, I am graceful to my wife, Nelle, and my daughter, Erika, for their encouragement and long-suffering.

Jeff Henderson

University of Central Arkansas

Acknowledgments

"Outline for 'The Warden,'" "Commentary on 'The King's Indian,'" excerpts from "Letter to Burton [Weber]," and incidental quotations from other material in the John Gardner Papers collection at the University of Rochester Library, © by Georges Borchardt, Inc., are printed by permission of the Estate of John Gardner and Georges Borchardt, Inc.

Excerpts from *On Becoming a Novelist* by John Gardner, © 1983 by the Estate of John Gardner, reprinted by permission of Harper & Row Publishers, Inc.

Excerpts from "An Interview with John Gardner" by Roni Natov and Geraldine DeLuca, © 1978 by *The Lion and the Unicorn*, reprinted by permission of the Johns Hopkins University Press.

Excerpts from "Modern Moralities for Children: John Gardner's Children's Books" by Geraldine DeLuca and Roni Natov, © 1982 by the Board of Trustees, Southern Illinois University, reprinted by permission of the publisher.

Excerpts from *Arches and Light: The Fiction of John Gardner* by David Cowart, © 1983 by the Board of Trustees, Southern Illinois University, reprinted by permission of the publisher.

Excerpts from *A World of Order and Light: The Fiction of John Gardner* by Gregory L. Morris, © 1984 by the University of Georgia Press, reprinted by permission.

Excerpts from "The Wound and the Albatross: John Gardner's Apprenticeship" by John M. Howell, © 1985 by John M. Howell, reprinted by permission of the author.

Part 1

THE SHORT FICTION

John Gardner and the Forms of Fiction

A tendency exists, even among serious students of John Gardner's fiction, to think of the canon of his works as comprising only the ten novels on which his fame as a writer chiefly rests. Thus the two major critical studies that have been published to date, David Cowart's *Arches and Light*[1] and Gregory Morris's *A World of Order and Light*[2] (both of them subtitled "The Fiction of John Gardner") scarcely even mention the epic poem *Jason and Medeia*,[3] which is certainly one of Gardner's major works of fiction. And while both these books devote a chapter to each of Gardner's collections of short fiction, it is clear enough that their authors think of Gardner is primarily a novelist, hardly a poet at all, and a writer of short stories perhaps only in his spare time. At least one senses something like such an attitude in, for example, Morris's reference to Gardner's 1981 collection *The Art of Living and Other Stories*[4] as a consolidation of the "random fiction" that Gardner "had floating about in various journals and magazines" and in his further characterization of this group of stories as "a working through of problematical parts of Gardner's past, a sort of therapy in prose by which Gardner comes to at least a temporary truce with private emotional bogies" (Morris, 184).[5]

Further confirmation of this lack of attention to Gardner's short fiction may be found by scanning any bibliography of critical commentary on Gardner's works. Such lists contain growing numbers of books and articles on the novels, but no books and very few articles that deal with Gardner's work in either poetry or short fiction. This neglect is understandable in view of the sheer volume of the novels in relation to the other works, but it is unfortunate insofar as it may foster an erroneous estimate of the importance of the poetry and short stories in the Gardner canon and, indeed, hinder their proper appreciation. The purpose of the present study is to counteract whatever critical neglect Gardner's short fiction may have suffered and to show that the stories, tales, and novellas indeed occupy a legitimate and important place in the body of Gardner's fiction.

Gardner was intensely interested in all the varieties and forms of fiction, from his various perspectives as artist, teacher, and critical theorist. As an author, he wrote examples of most of the different kinds of fiction commonly practiced by writers both of the present day and of the distant past. As a highly successful teacher of writing—and one who inspired discipular devotion among his students—he of course worked constantly with students' manuscripts of stories and novels of all types and lengths, and the thoroughness and insight of the commentaries and analyses he lavished on students' work are legendary.[6] As critic and theorist, Gardner's interest in the varieties of fiction spanned his entire career. It will be recalled that his first published book (coauthored with Lennis Dunlap) was a critical anthology of short fiction entitled *The Forms of Fiction*. Considering Gardner's strong sense of the distinctions among various fictional forms and the extreme care with which, as will be shown, he wrought those distinct forms in his own work, it seems reasonable to approach Gardner's short fiction in exactly the same spirit as his novels: that is, as the most carefully wrought and considered specimens of a particular literary species or subgenre that the author was capable of producing.

John Gardner's reputation as a writer of short fiction rests primarily upon the nineteen stories and tales, fourteen of them previously published in a variety of magazines and journals and one of them ("Vlemk the Box-Painter") previously published as a book, that Gardner included in the collections *The King's Indian: Stories and Tales* (1974)[7] and *The Art of Living and Other Stories* (1981). These stories and a few others (principally several excerpts from the novel-in-progress later published as *Nickel Mountain* and the posthumously published "Julius Caesar and the Werewolf")[8] constitute the body of work usually referred to as Gardner's adult short fiction. Such scant critical attention as Gardner's short stories have received has quite properly focused on these as most important, and so will the present study.

Gardner also published some twelve children's stories, all but two of them appearing for the first time in print in the three collections entitled *Dragon, Dragon and Other Tales* (1975), *Gudgekin the Thistle Girl and Other Tales* (1976), and *The King of the Hummingbirds and Other Tales* (1977).[9] These collections attracted considerable favorable notice (along with some unfavorable notice, as was the case with nearly everything Gardner published) from reviewers of children's books, and any full consideration of Gardner's work in short fiction must take these stories into account.

A study that attempts, as this one does, to analyze and evaluate a range of work as broad and various as Gardner's short fiction must deal with the problem of how to organize the discussion. An obvious principle of organization involves a thematic approach. The themes of Gardner's fiction, both long and short, are both conspicuous and well known. They include the fundamental tension between order and chaos, the redemptive power of love and art, the necessity of human community, the belief that life imitates art and that it is the value and function of art to clarify and improve life, and the possibility that people can attain "mundane salvation." A difficulty arises, however, when one attempts to arrange or organize Gardner's stories into these thematic categories. The problem is simply that, as virtually all critics of Gardner's fiction have observed, Gardner's vision and thematic concerns are remarkably consistent. As we shall see, nearly all the stories embody nearly all of the author's characteristic themes. A thematic arrangement of Gardner's stories would therefore be almost meaningless.

Another possible organizational principle suggests itself. From one perspective, it appears that Gardner wrote three kinds of stories: realistic stories in which characters, events, and the world they occur in are pretty much recognizable as people, events, and surroundings that the rest of us are normally familiar with (stories like "Pastoral Care," "The Joy of the Just," "Redemption," "Stillness," "Come on Back," "The Art of Living," etc.); so-called fabulations in which reality appears recognizable but strangely skewed, operating by different rules ("The Library Horror," "The Ravages of Spring," "The King's Indian," etc.); and fables or tales set in a more fantastic, almost fairy-tale world (the children's stories and such as the "Tales of Queen Louisa," "Vlemk the Box-Painter," and "Trumpeter"). Certainly these differences in levels of realistic representation must be recognized and dealt with, but to group the stories into such categories for discussion would, I believe, create more problems than it solved. Mainly, it would violate principles of organization the author himself imposed when he assembled and arranged his most important stories into *The King's Indian* and *The Art of Living*.

What makes the strongest claim as an ordering principle for discussion of the stories, it seems to me, is that organization and arrangement which Gardner created in the two collections. Not only did Gardner publish the title story for the first time in each collection, but in *The King's Indian* he added two more new stories ("Queen Louisa" and

5

"Muriel") and arranged the nine stories into three "books," called "The Midnight Reader," "Tales of Queen Louisa," and "The King's Indian," the last of which consists of the title story alone. And as we shall see, all ten of the stories in *The Art of Living*, in spite of the widest-imaginable apparent diversity among them, possess a thematic coherence that makes it difficult to believe they were written at such different times and, except for the title story, originally published independently of one another in various journals. There can be no doubt that Gardner carefully planned the arrangement of the stories in these collections, however various the circumstances of their individual composition may have been. It appears, therefore, that the most reasonable way to approach the stories critically may well be in the order in which they exist in the collections, and that is the approach this study will take.

The King's Indian: Stories and Tales

As a writer of short stories, John Gardner attracted little critical attention prior to the publication of his first collection of short fiction, *The King's Indian: Stories and Tales*, in November 1974. He was, however, already a famous writer by that time, having published five novels—*The Resurrection* (1966), *The Wreckage of Agathon* (1970), the award-winning *Grendel* (1971), the best-selling *The Sunlight Dialogues* (1972), and *Nickel Mountain* (1973)—and the masterly but critically ill received epic poem *Jason and Medeia* (1973). Undoubtedly, his reputation and popularity as a novelist helped convince his publisher (Knopf) to bring out a collection of his short stories.

Like most novelists, Gardner had written and published a number of short stories before achieving recognition as a writer. The earliest such publication seems to have been a story entitled "Freshman," published in 1952 in *Boulder*, a DePauw University campus magazine that listed Gardner (who was a student there at the time) as a member of its editorial staff. Other early short story publications included several pieces that later appeared as chapters or sections of the novel *Nickel Mountain* and one ("A Little Night Music") that Gardner later revised for inclusion in *The Sunlight Dialogues*.

It seems appropriate, however, to date the beginning of Gardner's career as an important short story writer from the publication of the stories he saw fit to include in *The King's Indian*. As mentioned previously, only the title story and two others ("Queen Louisa" and "Muriel") were printed for the first time in *The King's Indian*, although three others ("The Warden," "John Napper Sailing through the Universe," and "King Gregor and the Fool") were printed elsewhere during the same year (1974) the collection appeared. Stories published in earlier years include "Pastoral Care" (1972), "The Ravages of Spring" (1973), and "The Temptation of St. Ivo" (1972).[10]

Regardless of the times and circumstances of their original composition, the nine stories in *The King's Indian* possess a remarkable thematic coherence that could easily lead a reader to believe that all the stories were written with the intention of their being collected into a single book. And while this was apparently not the case, it is nevertheless true that the author was acutely conscious of the thematic connections and relationships among these stories and that he consciously grouped and arranged them. Gardner himself identified one common theme of the stories when he said, in a well-known interview with Marshall Harvey, that the "whole book [*The King's Indian*] is a study in aesthetics . . . in the only sense that really counts, as it expresses people through a theory of beauty"; he then cited the character Jonathan Upchurch in "The King's Indian" as "a model for all artists."[11] One of Gardner's most insistently recurrent themes has to do with the purpose and function of art and the character and responsibility of the artist, and so it is no surprise that this theme should be a prominent or even unifying principle among Gardner's stories. Indeed, we will see later that the same theme is of primary importance in Gardner's second collection of adult short stories, *The Art of Living*.

Gardner divided *The King's Indian* into three sections, or "books." The first, entitled "The Midnight Reader," includes five stories: "Pastoral Care," "The Ravages of Spring," "The Temptation of St. Ivo," "The Warden," and "John Napper Sailing through the Universe." This first section, as the title implies, contains in a figurative sense the darkest stories in the collection, at least prior to the last story, "John Napper Sailing through the Universe," which breaks through the threatening gloom of the earlier stories into the light. But even in the bleakest of the stories, which most readers would agree are "The Temptation of St. Ivo" and "The Warden," the darkness is not total. There is at least a glimmer of light, or the hope of one. Even when Gardner's vision is most grim, there is always the possibility of a rebirth, a resurrection, or the attainment of salvation. The second book, "Tales of Queen Louisa," includes "Queen Louisa," "King Gregor and the Fool," and "Muriel." Book 3 consists of the title story, or novella, "The King's Indian" alone. The following pages offer critical commentary on and interpretation of these stories. For other critics' views, the reader is referred to the notes to part 1 and to the reprints of other critics' works in part 3.

The Midnight Reader

As was the case with virtually every book John Gardner published, critical response to *The King's Indian* in the form of early reviews was mixed, though in the case of this book preponderantly favorable.[12] The first story in the collection, "Pastoral Care," is also the story reviewers most often singled out for special praise. Rod Cockshutt, for example, in his generally unfavorable review, cites this "straightforward and touching" story as the only admirable work in the collection, and Howard Derrickson, in a favorable review, praises both "Pastoral Care" and "The King's Indian" as "moral tales." Five other reviewers cite "Pastoral Care" as the "best" story in the collection, Roger Garfitt labeling it the "least fabulous," Minnie Hite Moody calling it the "simplest," William Parrill classing it among the "more realistic" stories, and Blanche H. Gelfant and Francis J. Thompson rating it simply "best." The lone dissenting opinion is that of Alan Friedman, who, while praising the story as "straightforward" and "enormously appealing," finds it ultimately "unsatisfying because it lacks the magic of the other, more fantastic tales."[13] Thus one critic dislikes the story for the very reason others find to praise it. Such polar diversity has not been unusual among critical responses, not only to Gardner's fiction, but to all his works.

"Pastoral Care" and the last of the five stories in book one of *The King's Indian*, "John Napper Sailing through the Universe," are certainly the most "realistic" stories in the collection, in the sense that their characters and incidents and the world in which they occur are pretty much recognizable as people, events, and surroundings most readers are normally familiar with. These two stories and others in Gardner's "realistic" mode (including most of the stories in the 1981 collection *The Art of Living*) contrast sharply in character, setting, and incident with the more "fabulous" stories—or "fabulations," as critics nowadays commonly call such fictions—in which reality appears recognizable but strangely skewed, often operating by different rules. The "fabulous" stories in *The King's Indian* include the title story, which by itself constitutes book three, as well as the other three stories in book one, "The Ravages of Spring," "The Temptation of St. Ivo," and "The Warden." Gardner also wrote a third type of story, which may be characterized as fantastic or fairy-tale-like. The three stories in book two fit this category, as do Gardner's stories for children and the novella "Vlemk the Box-Painter."

"Pastoral Care"

"Pastoral Care" is set mainly in Carbondale, Illinois, where Gardner lived and taught—at Southern Illinois University—from 1965 until the

early 1970s. This area of southern Illinois (specifically, a rural community located along the very real and splendidly named Boskydell
Road just south of Carbondale, where Gardner bought a large, old
farmhouse and lived during his tenure at SIU) also provides the setting
for two more of Gardner's stories, "The Ravages of Spring," which
follows "Pastoral Care" in *The King's Indian,* and "The Joy of the Just,"
which appears in *The Art of Living.* The central character in "Pastoral
Care," who also serves as the first-person, present-tense narrator, is the
Reverend Eugene Pick, the relatively young, unmarried, bearded minister of a Presbyterian church in Carbondale. The time is the middle
or late 1960s, during the Vietnam War, when student unrest, including
destructive riots, bombings, and the burning of buildings, was all too
common at universities across the country. Carbondale suffered perhaps more than its share of such activity, supposedly because of the
presence at the university of a "Center for Vietnamese Studies." In
any case, there were destructive riots on the campus and along the
main business streets of Carbonale and at least rumors of plots to bomb
university buildings, including, supposedly, a women's dormitory.
While I am not aware that any buildings were actually blown up (as the
Art Building is in "Pastoral Care"), the university did eventually lose
its Old Main building to fire. Against this backdrop of social unrest and
threatened upheaval, the Reverend Pick attempts to shepherd his ag-
ing, conservative, diminishing flock into the radical perceptions and
insights with which he sympathizes. In this he fails, but he does succeed, at least indirectly, in getting the police station and his own
church bombed and in very nearly destroying himself.

Since the narration flows through Pick's consciousness, we are aware
of his thoughts, feelings, and attitudes. We see that he is, like most of
Gardner's protagonists, intelligent, highly introspective, and basically
well intentioned. He is given to self-analysis and seems, rather smugly,
to think he understands himself pretty well. He is, he thinks, genuinely concerned for the spiritual (or psychological) well-being of his
congregation, and we see him in several instances ministering to their
needs, fulfilling his responsibility to provide "pastoral care." He recalls, in a flashback, his counseling of elderly Miss Ellis, a piano
teacher, in her spiritual crisis brought on by disillusionment regarding
the effects of foreign missions, which have always been the principal
focus for her religious feelings. She is near despair when Pick kneels
and prays with her in his study, beneath the battered sign on the wall
that says "THE CHURCHES OF CARBONDALE WELCOME YOU." (The

sign's message is quoted four times in the story and serves as an ironic counterpoint to the story's events.) Conscious that he is manipulating the woman psychologically, Pick sings a hymn with her and assures her that Jesus understands and loves her and that all will be well. On his part this is pure hypocrisy. He feels contempt for her theology as well as what he imagines are her childlike mental processes.

When they stand and she thanks him profusely for his spiritual help, he replies, "Don't thank me, Miss Ellis, thank Our Savior." Thank the Masked Man, he might just as sincerely have said. Pick does acknowledge that his response is patronizing but denies that it is "callous": "I prefer to view it as a momentary lapse from charity. Love is a difficult thing to sustain without hypocrisy on the one hand, stupidity on the other. I felt sympathy for her, but not enough sympathy to abandon my theology, accept her as an equal" (*KI*, 10).

In another flashback the minister recalls his first pastoral encounter with John Grewy, M.D., an elder in the church and the man who some years earlier was responsible for the building fund drive that resulted in the church's expanded "physical plant," as he calls it. Grewy is stodgy and conservative in his social and political views—thus earning his radical minister's contempt—but he is sincerely religious, and he is spiritually anguished when he visits Pick and expresses his fear that he may somehow "lack the *intelligence* to be a Christian," "whooping," as Pick styles it, "God help me! God help me! . . . Lost! . . . Lost!" (*KI*, 13). Pick consoles Elder Grewy, much as he had consoled Miss Ellis and with much the same air of smug superiority and self-satisfaction.

We also glimpse the Reverend Pick counseling married women from the congregation: "dowdy, fat Carol Ann Watson," who is having an affair and feels guilty because she doesn't feel guilty about the affair (Pick jokingly suggests that perhaps she should have two affairs), and the much more attractive Marilyn Fish, toward whom Pick entertains lecherous longings and who is also having an affair—with the same man as the other woman (but at a later time), church member Levelsmacher, whom Pick despises, partly for reasons he understands and partly for reasons he does not understand. Pick's insight into his own motives has blind spots.

In all these instances of "pastoral care," Pick's motives are tainted—corrupted, even—by his selfish concerns. Even if his counseling seems to help those who receive it, Pick himself remains in dire spiritual straits, like Chaucer's Pardoner, who, although a "ful vicious man" himself, can nevertheless cause others to turn from sin by his eloquent preaching. But the Pardoner is surely damned, if anyone is, and the Reverend Pick will soon find himself in grave need of salvation. A measure of Pick's egotism may be seen in his reaction to Dr. Grewy's presence in his office, counting the collection plate money from the service just concluded. Silently observing Grewy's appearance, Pick thinks that Grewy would "do well to grow a beard, in my opinion. Nevertheless, God loves him, and even I, I find, am glad, as usual, to see him" (*KI*, 11). *Even I?* The reader senses that, for all his introspection, Pick is only partially conscious of the irony in this remark. His mental state transcends mere egotism to achieve hubris.

While Pick's early attempts at pastoral care seem successful (though poisoned at their source by his selfishness), he utterly fails the most important test of his ministerial responsibility. This test comes in the form of a visitor to his church—a wild-eyed, bearded, fatigues-clad, obviously radical and probably mad young man who appears one Sunday near the back of the church. His unfamiliar, "ghostly face, bearded, prophetically staring" (*KI*, 8), unnerves Pick, winding up his sermon, and causes him to lose his place, repeat himself. As the congregation files out, Pick comes face to face with the hippie visitor, who he assumes must be a college student. Reaching to shake hands, Pick "inadvertently, unless *he* arranged it" (*KI*, 10) catches the young man's thumb and finds himself participating in a "power-to-the-people" handshake. Of course the young man "arranged" the handshake, as the reader recognizes more readily than Pick does. Not only is the young man a hippie and a radical, but, as we learn later, he has been to Vietnam. It's the only way he could possibly shake hands.

That Pick misses the handshake is an indication that he is as much an outsider with the radical element as he is with his own congregation. The young man stares at Pick and doesn't speak, backing out of the church. Pick concludes that he is undoubtedly "a maniac, or else stoned. Or Christ come down to check on me" (*KI*, 10). The minister is momentarily alarmed at this last thought (which is closer to the truth than he can guess), but the feeling passes and Pick dismisses it as "of no importance," admitting that he has "no idea why the stranger rouses such feelings in me" (*KI*, 11).

Dr. Grewy seems to have a sincere affection for the minister. Twice, Grewy tries to warn Pick to be more discreet in his sermons and associations. The first warning reveals something of the content of Pick's sermons when Grewy says, hesitantly, "You should be careful what you say. Overthrowing governments and things, I mean. What if someone from the FBI . . ." (*KI*, 14). Pick has evidently been advocating violence and insurrection from his pulpit, carried away on some manic ego trip. It would be hard to imagine a less appropriate or effective pastoral approach to that particular audience. Presumably, the only receptive ears in the house belonged to the radical visitor.

We learn later that Pick's remarks did indeed impress the visitor: "Your sermon really blew my mind," he says later, when he and Pick finally converse (*KI*, 21). Following his friendly admonition, Grewy asks Pick if he's heard the news that "someone blew up the Art Building" at the university. Pick receives the information with less concern than he would show over a fender bender in the church parking lot: "'That's terrible,' I say, and look at my watch. 'But we'd better go, Dr. Grewy. Actually, I'm starving'" (*KI*, 14). As they leave the church office, Pick recalls, with self-righteous disapproval, Grewy's work with the building fund that resulted in the church's new additions.

In Pick's view, Grewy had "bowed down . . . to the brass god Stewardship," although he "meant no harm" by it. He thinks of Grewy's donating his services to the free health clinic and the drug crisis center and concludes, with unconscious irony, that while Grewy "may not be exactly the salt of the earth . . . he's as good a man as he knows how to be" (*KI*, 15). Gardner expects the reader to recognize that Pick is dead wrong. Grewy *is* the salt of the earth, if anyone is, and at this point he is a far better man than Pick, who is far worse than he "knows how to be."

The inevitable meeting between Pick and the young radical is set up by Marilyn Fish, the attractive blonde whom Pick lusts after. Visiting in Pick's office, Marilyn tells him that she sent the boy to his church. She had met him through her volunteer work in the drug clinic and sees him as "a sweet, gentle boy," though a "little crazy, of course," and "into revolution." She tells him also that the boy was impressed by Pick's sermon and wants to talk with him sometime. She will send him to Pick (*KI*, 20).

The boy appears in Pick's office, providing the minister with an opportunity to give pastoral care to the only real congregation he has. Pick fails miserably to give anything. His entire contribution to the conversation consists of the remarks "It was wonderful to have you with us," "I'm Reverend Pick," "I don't believe—," "Tao?" (a mistaken repetition of the boy's name, which he says is Dow, as in "Dow Chemical Company"), "You're a student at the university?" "You really bomb things?" "Of course," and "I'm not sure what you mean" (*KI*, 21–23).

The scene is three pages long, more than half of it taken up with Pick's silent reflections and the remarks just quoted. The rest is what the boy says. Pick's sermon has "blown his mind"; he was a student but was drafted and sent to Vietnam; now he's "into revolution" and "bomb[s] things" but not people. It is clear enough that he bombed the Art Building, as it is clear that Pick has reinforced his revolutionary zeal and inspired him to further incendiary acts. When the boy leaves, Pick follows him, belatedly, but cannot catch him, thus losing any opportunity to intervene in the boy's behavior.

The interview has evidently been overheard by Pick's secretary, Janice, and Sylvester, the janitor—a circumstance that leads to Grewy's second warning to Pick. After a church business meeting, Grewy, again hesitantly and with apparent goodwill, tells Pick that "certain people" have overheard the conversation, and he expresses his wish that the minister be "more discreet" (*KI*, 24–25). Pick's response, predictably, is to become angry and defensive. He makes a mental note to fire both secretary and custodian and immediately begins plotting his next sermon, which will be, in effect, an act of vengeance.

The Reverend Pick delivers the sermon of his life. It might be called his fig-tree sermon from its central image, the tree cursed by Jesus to eternal barrenness for failing to bear figs when Jesus wanted them. Pick argues that the "fig tree represents dead, sham religion, authority grown sick" (*KI*, 27), and by a remarkably convoluted sequence of exegesis and scriptural cross-reference he concludes that the meaning of the fig tree "parable" is that if the government is immoral, we should "blow up the Pentagon" (*KI*, 28).[14] During the sermon, Pick has noted with relief that the bearded revolutionary does not seem to be in attendance. If he had been, Pick might have softened his remarks somewhat. The boy is in fact present, though, and Pick sees him during his concluding prayer, lurking in the vestibule. He's heard it all.

When next we see the Reverend Pick he is on a train passing through Ohio in the night, in severe distress. Although he tries, feebly, to deny it, he knows that he has fled his pastoral responsibility—indeed, all responsibility. He carries a two-day-old Carbondale newspaper with the headline "BOMB DAMAGES POLICE STATION" and the subhead ' Bomber linked to local minister" (*KI*, 29). A fellow passenger introduces himself to Pick as a physician (a ghastly doppelgänger for Dr. Grewy, who Pick fleetingly imagines may be pursuing him), comments on the Carbondale bombing (a "terrible business"), and asks Pick if he's heard the latest on that story: "The crazy nut's blown up some church. I saw it on television" (*KI*, 30).

Pick is brought close to the bottom of the existential pit by the knowledge of his responsibility and his fleeing from that responsibility. He is haunted momentarily by the image of the barren fig tree and his sense of identification with the "dead, sham religion" it represents to him. He drifts toward nihilism (the greatest of evils, in Gardner's view) and the abandonment of all hope, all mission, in his flight to existential freedom. The story approaches a thematic climax in the conflict between order and disorder, a principal theme of this story, as it is, indeed, of Gardner's fiction generally. Characters, events, and institutions in this story may be seen as representing the opposing principles. For example, the buildings that the radical former student bombs (the Art Building, the police station, and Pick's Presbyterian church) are all societal manifestations of the principle of order.

Like many Gardner characters, Pick is torn between the desire for the security of orderliness and regulation in his life and the lure of total, if absurd, freedom offered by nihilistic existentialism. This freedom can be had, however, only at the cost of despair. Pick is falling, in the terms of Gardner's fiction, into a kind of damnation. Symbolically, he is on a hell-bound train. As if it were an ultimately absurd insult, the physician he has just met makes a homosexual pass at him.

Pick's fall is interrupted by the train's halting suddenly in an emergency stop. As passengers and crew stumble out and along the tracks, Pick and the physician come to the scene of the accident. A pregnant hippie girl, stoned, has fallen off the train and been killed. Her companion, a "gigantic" bearded young man, kneels over her in an agony of grief, raging. It is too late for the doctor's skills: "We don't need a doctor, we need a priest!" the young man shouts. He is so large and crazed with grief, and no doubt drug crazed as well, that no one will approach him. The situation presents Pick with a last, desperate chance for redemption, salvation. He takes the opportunity this time, although not by conscious choice; he is unable to help himself. He approaches the grieving man, identifying himself as "a minister" and afraid, momentarily, that the man will "charge" him. "But there is nothing to charge. I am no one, for the moment; a disembodied voice; God's minister" (*KI*, 34). The man responds, weeping.

This is Pick's salvation. To attain it, he must annihilate self (become "no one") and act with godlike—not hubristic, but disinterested—

affirmation, which he has apparently never done before. It has been a long fall, and Pick, like other Gardner characters (Peter Mickelsson, for instance, in the novel *Mickelsson's Ghosts*), must endure a kind of death—death of self—before his psychic resurrection is possible. The situation of a character who, pushed to or beyond despair and in the Siren-like grip of nihilism, narrowly achieves redemption through annihilation of self is a familiar one in Gardner's fiction.

"The Ravages of Spring"

Appropriately, "The Ravages of Spring" was first published in the magazine *Fantastic Science Fiction and Fantasy Stories* (April 1973); the story possesses some standard features of both the science fiction and fantasy subgenres: a mad scientist, his laboratory and equipment, and vague "scientific" underpinnings for his work, as well as the fantasy elements of hints of the supernatural and inexplicable, and an atmosphere of gothic horror. Like "Pastoral Care," "The Ravages of Spring" is set in southern Illinois, although the time is perhaps three-quarters of a century earlier. The precise time setting cannot be determined, but internal evidence points strongly to sometime during the last two decades of the nineteenth century. According to the narrator, the mad scientist, Professor Hunter, speaks of one of Lamarck's ideas as "old," and, more tellingly, mentions "some monk who had recently gotten some curious information from beans—or perhaps from peas; I've forgotten" (*KI*, 54). Lamarck died in 1829, and the "monk" is of course Gregor Mendel, who died in 1884. The reference to Mendel's work as "recent" suggests a date not long after 1884, and the fact that the narrator, an unusually well read man of science himself, has obviously never heard of Mendel or his work indicates a date earlier than 1900, when Mendel's work was brought to popular attention.[15]

Like many of Gardner's narrators, that of "The Ravages of Spring" is a fascinating character. Gardner takes some pains to establish the credibility and reliability of the narrator by making him not only intelligent, well educated, and a member of a profession that traditionally inspires confidence (a physician), but a plain, blunt man of common sense and honest, realistic, steady vision as well—"as plain a man as was ever set to toiling and grieving on this godforsaken planet; a bachelor; a reader of dull books; a country doctor" (*KI*, 35), as he describes himself. He is quick to point out the contrast between his down-to-earth reasonableness and the wild tale he has to tell—"a tale at first glance more fit for the author of 'The Raven' or . . . 'Ulalume'" (*KI*, 35). He is not, he says, a Platonist like Poe, he judges "absolute values" primarily by their lack of favorable effect on the digestion, and he (again unlike the Platonists) prefers present time to eternity, although he does like "things done properly—even tortuously, when that's what's required—but done by a man who's got one ear cocked toward the infinite" (*KI*, 35–36).

This last detail—the image of the ear cocked toward the infinite—interestingly undercuts the narrator's anti-Platonist claims. He is willing to listen to the infinite, at least, although he claims to prefer the temporal. A later development in the story casts further doubt on his honesty and directness, when he gives a phony name ("Dr. William Thorpe") to his host and hostess at the mad scientist's house, where he has sought shelter from a tornado. Not only that, but he never reveals his real name to the reader, either. While this perhaps does not make "Thorpe" an unreliable narrator, it should nevertheless serve notice to the reader that it may be risky to take everything he says at face value.

In large outline, the plot of "The Ravages of Spring" is quite simple. The country doctor–narrator, making his rounds to call on his patients one June day, in his buggy drawn by his horse Shakespeare (presumably the animal's real name), must seek shelter from multiple (three) tornados at the eerie, isolated house occupied, he finds, by a man who claims to be Professor John Hunter and an apparently younger woman Hunter insists is his mother. Thorpe recognizes Hunter's name as that of a notorious mad geneticist "dead [executed?] these thirty years and entombed with his victims" (*KI*, 51). Details remain sketchy about the "original" Professor Hunter, but the reader infers that he was regarded as a mad mass murderer (or abortionist, perhaps), as the narrator alludes to his "history of laboratory murders—grave on grave of dead foetuses" (*KI*, 52). The events of the story shed new light on the nature and origin of those "murdered" fetuses in the original Hunter's laboratory: they were his early failures in attempting human cloning. Eventually, Hunter evidently succeeded in cloning himself and his mother, or possibly his wife; the precise relationship is unclear, as the present Hunter refers to the woman as "my mother, my wife, my sister." It is clear that they are first- or second-generation clones of the original Hunter and his mother or wife: "We're not *human*, Dr. Thorpe. We're *copies!*—*klones!*" the mad Hunter exclaims to the disbelieving narrator (*KI*, 55), and insists that Thorpe accompany him and the woman to the tower room where his laboratory is located, to see the "proof" of his story.

Thorpe goes, reluctantly, and is treated to an array of machines, "great, square, black boxes over operating tables, glass-walled vats, cramped chemicals and tubing." This is Hunter's "ungodly" laboratory; outside the window the storm rages and the sky is "the unholy purple of glass balls on a lightning rod" (*KI*, 56). The setting—both storm and paraphernalia—could have been borrowed from a 1930s Frankenstein movie. As Hunter turns the crank on one of the infernal machines, and sparks fly, the tornadoes arrive, no longer three but four of them now, looming above the tower, "creatures more terrible than the Bible's Four Horsemen" and making a roar that the woman identifies as the voice of God, as she interprets the writhing black funnels as the ministers of divine wrath: "They've come! The Hounds of Heaven have found us! Forgive us, Thorpe!" (*KI*, 57).

The tornadoes completely destroy the tower and partially destroy the rest of the house. Thorpe is knocked unconscious and suffers a severe concussion, which, along with his earlier "fainting" episode upon arriving at the house, must cast some doubt on the accuracy of his perceptions of events. When he awakens he discovers that the laboratory, its machines, all of Hunter's papers, and indeed the bodies of Hunter and the woman are gone, carried off by the storm. The narrator remembers that he saw, or thought he saw, just before losing consciousness, Hunter's dying body "separate" into "several small creatures, pink, blue, green" (*KI*, 58). His uncertainty about the validity of this memory introduces a further ambiguity: are the three children Thorpe later finds in the storm cellar developments from these "fragments" of Hunter's body, or are they previously created clones? Morris concludes that they "are the pink and blue and green sparkles given off by Hunter in his death throe" (Morris, 123), but this notion seems unlikely. (Morris also has the narrator finding the children in the well rather than the storm cellar.)

Whatever Thorpe's bizarre memory may signify, it appears more probable that the children were there all the time. Earlier, when Thorpe urged that they all go to the storm cellar for safety, Hunter and the woman both said, falsely, that it was flooded and unusable, apparently to conceal the children's presence there. The only evidence that any of these events actually happened is a photograph of the original John Hunter that Thorpe later finds in his pocket (where he had absentmindedly placed it when his host showed it to him) and the existence of the three small children he finds in the storm cellar when he comes to. They are all "red-headed, buck-toothed, and pale as ghosts" (*KI*, 59). Only after the children have been placed in the temporary care of an elderly widow and "sometime midwife" does the doctor realize that these children must be "Klones! . . . all three of them, John Hunter cruelly resurrected" (*KI*, 65).

Spiritual or psychological resurrection or redemption of a character is one of Gardner's most insistently recurrent themes. As we saw in the discussion of "Pastoral Care," this redemption is typically achieved through an annihilation of self that allows the character to think and act from a position beyond personal involvement, with the disinterested affirmation that in Gardner's fiction is an attribute of the "god-like" state. In the literal, physical resurrection of John Hunter we see a horrible perversion of the redemptive process. Far from being transcended or eradicated, "self" is the element that is perpetuated, increasingly, with each successive cloning. As the present Hunter says, his mind contains fleeting memories of people who died a hundred years before. And although one of the three children dies when the old midwife lowers them in a tub into a well in a witchlike attempt to cure them of their apparent madness, two of them survive in the care of Dr. Thorpe.

As the story ends, the narrator drives the children home, talking to his horse "of animals, and monsters, and the nature of things" (*KI*, 68). The dawn sky is green, the air is unnaturally calm, and the birds have stopped singing. More tornadoes, more "ravages of spring" are in the offing.

As previously noted, "The Ravages of Spring" belongs to the category of Gardner's stories that may be called fabulations—stories in which the ordinary standards of realism, including our normal assumptions regarding time and space, do not necessarily apply. Thus there may be dreamlike, surrealistic sequences, such as the scene just following the clones' rescue from the well (*KI*, 67–68), strange interpenetrations among different times, and bizarre improbabilities in the world of natural phenomena—four tornadoes in a tight group, for instance.

The weird interpenetration of different times takes form as an influence of a later time on an earlier. When Thorpe regains consciousness after "fainting" just as he reached the shelter of the Hunter house, he sees Hunter, "aware, at first, only of red, red hair sweeping out . . . as ferocious and unnatural as the hair on an antique ventriloquist's dummy" (*KI*, 48). In a way, the comparison with a ventriloquist's dummy is not inappropriate for the clone, but Thorpe does not know about clones at the time. It is as if his future knowledge influences his perceptions. As his eyes focus, he sees that Hunter has "no ordinary face. Enormous gazelle eyes as pale as glass, an uptilted nose above protruding, crooked teeth, and skin very nearly as ashen as dried-out clay . . . a kind of face you'd not expect to see twice on one planet" (*KI*, 49). Again, there is an anticipatory irony in the notion of seeing this face twice; he will in fact see it five times; in the daguerreotype of the original Hunter, in the present Hunter, and in the three clone-children. But the primary ancestor of this distinctive face is, I suspect, actually a "ventriloquist's dummy": Edgar Bergen's Mortimer Snerd, I think, although a case might be made for the television puppet Howdy Doody as well.[16]

One important attribute of Gardner's fiction is his use of what he called a collage technique. By this he meant his appropriation and use of other writers' works, or parts of works, both in style and in substance. Gardner used this technique frequently, to the extent that a typical Gardner novel or story will have numerous "sources," both ancient and contemporary. Although Gardner readily acknowledged, in interviews and elsewhere, his literary borrowings, reviewers nevertheless occasionally charged him with virtual plagiarism. As Gardner saw it, however, he was merely working in a very old literary tradition that regards the whole world of literature—plots, characters, styles—as the common property (or at least fair game) of all practicing writers. This is, after all, the way Chaucer and Shakespeare came by most of their characters and plots. The author who uses others' material will not succeed, of course, if he merely copies—clones—the original. He must transform or transmute the material into something fresh and new by the synthesizing power of his own imagination and skill, as Chaucer and Shakespeare and, Gardner would insist, all the great writers did. Gardner worked in the same ways.

Thus it is that in "The Ravages of Spring" there are obvious and acknowledged echoes of Poe. The narrator himself draws the comparison when he characterizes his tale as "more fit for the author of 'The Raven'" (*KI*, 35). Yet the story is not merely an imitation of Poe, because other influences are at least as prominent—for instance, the movie tradition of mad scientists' laboratories and some of the conventions of science fiction. One might assume in this connection that Gardner capitalized on the popularity of the "cloning" idea, both in science fiction and in what might be called speculative biology, but as

Cowart points out, Gardner's cloning story was published before Ira Levin's novel about cloning Hitler, *The Boys from Brazil* (1976), and David M. Rorvik's nonfictional study *In His Image: The Cloning of a Man* (1978) (Cowart, 81). Nancy Freedman's novel about the cloning of President John F. Kennedy, *Joshua Son of None* (1973), appeared in the same year Gardner's story was originally published, but considering the early date for the story (April), it seems unlikely that Gardner would have been familiar with Freedman's novel.

Yet another literary presence that informs this story, from beginning to end, is that of Franz Kafka. Although the story is not what one would call Kafkaesque in any pervasive sense (as the later story "The Warden" assuredly is), "The Ravages of Spring" both begins and ends with evocations of Kafka's story "Ein Landarzt" ("A Country Doctor"). The narrator, like Kafka's, who also remains unnamed, twice identifies himself as "a country doctor" (Kafka's title) in the story's opening paragraphs, and in a sense Gardner's Dr. Thorpe actually is Kafka's Landarzt, kidnapped or shanghaied into another story and forced to function there, willy-nilly. Gardner pays his respects, as it were, to Kafka in the story's penultimate scene, where Thorpe ministers to the surviving clones he's rescued from the well:

> As the [lamp] flame leaped up, I reached toward the two who were living, to move them away, a little, from the corpse. As my hands drew near, their tiny mad eyes snapped suddenly into focus and their hands reached out to catch hold of me. I jerked back as I would if those wrinkled white hands were snakeheads. The old woman bent close—watching me, not the children—and though tears ran down her cheeks like rain, the evil, toothless mouth seemed to be smiling. Shakespeare had his head in the open door, silently urging me to hurry, there was very little time. A tingle of fear came over me, one that I remembered. I glanced around the table to see what I'd spilled or disturbed, but there was nothing, which faintly puzzled me. I concentrated again on the pitiful creatures. Their hands were raised, waiting, and their eyes had me nailed as a cat's eyes nail a mouse before she strikes. My mind was full of wind, reeling and shrieking, but the whole world outside was calm, waiting without hope or plan, with the vast and sorrowful gentleness of a deathly sick horse. (*KI*, 68)

The scene is pure imitation Kafka in its surreal quality and in Gardner's having the doctor's horse stick its head into the house, as Kafka's doctor's horses stick their heads through the window in the final scene of his story. Like Kafka's doctor, Thorpe is baffled but tries to behave rationally in an irrational situation. Gardner, and Kafka before him, may well have intended this situation as a symbolic representation of the human condition.

"The Temptation of St. Ivo"

In October 1977, Gardner participated in a symposium entitled "Signs and Symbols in Chaucer's Poetry" at the University of Alabama at Tuscaloosa. Gardner made two presentations, one a scholarly paper on Chaucer and the other a public reading from his fiction.[17] The reading, an evening event, was much different from the scholarly presentation. In a nearly packed auditorium, Gardner appeared on stage dressed in black trousers and a red tunic with an elaborately embroidered golden dragon on the front. Appropriately (but also dangerously) before an audience composed largely of medieval scholars, he read the story "The Temptation of St. Ivo," introducing it with a jocular—rather than defiant—challenge: "I defy anyone to tell me what this story means," he said. When the reading ended, no one did so. Members of the learned audience did, however, point out what appeared to be certain failures of accuracy in detail. One questioned Gardner's use of a simile involving potatoes, in which the character Brother Ivo says his "arms and legs are like a sickly old woman's, as white as potato sprouts under the cassock" (*KI*, 70), on the ground that potatoes were unknown in Europe at the time when the story presumably takes place.

Another member of the audience pointed out a similar anachronism by noting that the style of manuscript illumination practiced by Brother Ivo and the presence of a knight in armor such as appears in the story's last scene are temporally incompatible. Gardner received these quibbles with characteristic equanimity, remarking something like "Interesting" or "Good point." It seems likely that these anachronisms do represent lapses of some sort on the author's part, but it must also be noted that this story is one of Gardner's fabulations rather than one of his realistic stories, and the ordinary restrictions of time and space do not necessarily apply.

Of more importance is the question of what the story means. The author's challenge to that particular audience to interpret the story surely was not an indication that the story has no meaning, but rather that the story is unusually intricate and difficult. "The Temptation of

St. Ivo" is set in a medieval monastery, and except for other monks who move in the background, there are only three characters: Ivo (the narrator); his nemesis, Brother Nicholas; and an anonymous knight-errant who appears in the final scene. As at least two reviewers noticed, the setting and the opposition between two monks are reminiscent of Browning's "The Soliloquy of the Spanish Cloister." James G. Murray, reviewing *The King's Indian* in the journal *Critic*, lists Browning as "one of Gardner's sources," and Keith Neilson, in his commentary in *Masterplots Annual 1975*, specifically cites Browning's "Soliloquy" as a probable source.[18] Such is undoubtedly the case.

Early manuscript versions of this story, located in the Gardner Papers collection at the University of Rochester Library, show that Gardner had originally named Ivo "Brother Lawrence" (the name of the monk who is the object of the speaker's hatred in Browning's poem.)[19] Brother Nicholas's name in these same early drafts was "Oliver," although of course the speaker in Browning's poem is unnamed. While it seems clear that Browning did provide part of the initial impetus for Gardner's story, primarily in setting and in Ivo's "saintly" character and his antagonist's viciousness, it must be noted that Gardner's story is not merely an expanded dramatization of Browning's poem; or if it is, the situation and the characters' motives are much altered and apparently rendered much more complex.

Thematically, "The Temptation of St. Ivo" covers familiar ground. Representatives of order and anarchy (Ivo and Nicholas, respectively) are thrown against each other in a battle of nihilistic despair against affirmation and hope, in which the stakes are redemption and salvation. In different terms, the story reenacts the conflict between the Reverend Pick and the anarchist bomber in "Pastoral Care" and that between Thorpe and Hunter in "The Ravages of Spring," as well as similar oppositions in Gardner's novels—for example, Grendel vs. the Shaper in *Grendel*, the Sunlight Man vs. Chief Clumly in *The Sunlight Dialogues*, Bishop Brask vs. Lars-Goren in *Freddy's Book*—and in other stories examined later in part 1. This characteristic conflict often appears in Gardner's fiction as a struggle between "good art" and "bad art," or between the "good artist" and the "bad artist." For Gardner, "good art" is that which affirms, clarifies, and enhances life, while "bad art" is that which denies and degrades life by advocating nihilism and despair. In "The Temptation of St. Ivo" the opponents are both artists, illuminators of manuscripts.

Ivo is an immensely talented artist, by common consent a genius at the illumination of manuscripts. Like Browning's Andrea del Sarto, he is a "faultless painter." He has spent his life "serving God" by drawing "zoomorphic capitals—beasts eating beasts in the universal war of raging will against raging will: dragons, bears, birds, rabbits, bucks, all coiled, unwitting, in the larger design of an *A* or an *O*"—a design that represents the totality and the order of creation, the "Alpha and Omega" (*KI*, 70). That is, Ivo affirms with every stroke of his pen and brush his unquestioning belief in the divinely ordained and ordered universe of his religious faith. As a Gardnerian artist, however, he is incomplete. He has not stood at the rim of the existential pit and stared into the "darkness at the heart of things." Until he does this, comes face to face with the threat of meaninglessness in an "abandoned universe" and overcomes the temptation of despair and the lure of nihilistic "freedom," he will not be able to affirm life truly and authoritatively.

Brother Nicholas, a new arrival at the monastery, is also a manuscript artist of considerable talent, but he is the Gardnerian type of the "bad artist." His work is sloppy and careless because he has succumbed to the doctrines of nihilism. "*Nothing means anything,*" he continually whispers, in one guise or another, to Brother Ivo, and his shoddy work as an artist proclaims the same message. He is the agent of Ivo's temptation, relentlessly pursuing him, whispering constantly in violation of the rule of silence, taunting Ivo and urging him to abandon his "absurd" rules and speak. Ivo resists, clinging to his belief in divine order and in the rightness and sanctity of the rules, but an anguished conflict grows in his mind.

In an attempt to flee his nemesis, Ivo requests a transfer to the monastery fields. But Nicholas follows him, continuing his assault: "*Brother Ivo, your rules are absurd! The order of the world is an accident. We could change it in an instant, simply by opening our throats and speaking. Brother Ivo, listen!*" (*KI*, 75). The ultimate temptation comes when Nicholas tells Ivo that he has discovered the lair of the phoenix and intends to leave the monastery at night and murder the creature, and only Ivo can save it.

In the privacy of the confessional booth, Ivo discusses the matter with the confessor, who suggests that, as Ivo has suspected, Nicholas's behavior may be some devious plea for help, that he may be an anguished soul himself, in which case Ivo might be obliged to break monastic rules in the name of a higher good, to minister to Nicholas's spiritual needs. But, of course, it may be a satanic temptation instead.

The confessor also suggests that Nicholas may well mean something symbolic by "the Phoenix"—that "he's resolved to kill some child or virgin—a Phoenix in the sense of unique innocence and beauty. Or he may mean the Phoenix as figure of man's immortal soul—his own, perhaps . . . or yours. Then again, the Phoenix may be a symbol of Mary, as we read in Jerome, or of Christ Himself" (*KI*, 81). If Nicholas does in fact leave the monastery that night, the confessor continues, Ivo will have a "terrible choice" to make. The terror and necessity of that choice are not diminished by the fact that the confessor turns out to be Nicholas himself.

Nicholas does leave the monastery, and Ivo abandons the rules and follows him into the dark and trackless woods populated by boars, wolves, and perhaps more dangerous creatures. Lost and terrified, feeling abandoned and near despair, Ivo meets a knight in armor who befriends him and takes him onto his horse. They will confront together whatever horrors the forest holds. Sensing a presence, the knight hurls his dagger into the trees, but they "do not hear it strike, consumed by moss, dead trees, the darkness at the heart of things" (*KI*, 89).

Gardner's original title for this story was "The Phoenix," which is a measure of the importance of the phoenix element in the story. In addition to the symbolic values for the mythical bird enumerated by Nicholas in his guise as the confessor, the phoenix more generally is a symbol for resurrection or redemption. Here, the phoenix represents whatever it is that can be lost or killed by nihilistic despair, namely the affirmative and redemptive power of art that confronts the "darkness at the heart of things," takes note of it, and affirms in spite of it or in opposition to it, even though the odds may be, as the knight says, "a hundred to zero." The knight, like Beowulf in Gardner's novel *Grendel*, is the hero who embodies and executes the values inculcated by the true artist. Indeed, the three characters of this story are analogous to Grendel (the Sartrean nihilist, like Nicholas), the Shaper (the true artist, like Ivo), and Beowulf (the hero). Ivo, by choosing to leave the naïve security of his rules without falling to the lure of nihilism, becomes that true artist, becomes a saint.

"The Warden"

"Nobody I know of writes books *quite* so carefully organized," Gardner said in an interview with Ed Christian.[20] The remark refers to Gardner's practice of constructing stories in which every detail, every image, every nuance of characterization, dialogue, and description contributes to a structure as intricately coherent and controlled as the illuminated capitals in Brother Ivo's manuscripts. This is the way Gardner worked, and the result is, typically, a story or novel in which every element—virtually every lexical word—has a calculated bearing on the story's theme, meaning, or aesthetic effect. "The Warden," the next-to-last (and darkest, most puzzling and disturbing) story in the "Midnight Reader" section of *The King's Indian*, illustrates Gardner's penchant for this kind of artistic "organization" better than most others, principally because Gardner left among his papers a two page handwritten analysis of the story (Gardner Papers, box B-11). Although it is uncertain whether Gardner's commentary on "The Warden" is in the nature of an outline he made while planning the story or an analysis he abstracted from the story after he had written it, the former seems much more probable, considering that Gardner often made outlines of plots he was working on.[21] A summary of this outline will shed more light on what the story means and how it works than any amount of critical commentary could.

Generally, it may be noted that "The Warden," like "The Ravages of Spring," owes a debt to Kafka. In this story the Kafkaesque elements are more diffuse than the specific borrowings we saw in "The Ravages of Spring." They include the setting in an apparently eastern European, totalitarian, impersonal, bureaucratic state where citizens are imprisoned on vague or unspecified charges, where all attempts to communicate with the bureaucracy or its representatives are frustrated, and where characters are required to function in absurd situations. Conditions continually deteriorate, and for most characters there seems little hope for improvement.

Gardner's notes indicate that he saw as a central conflict in "The Warden" the tension between the desire to be "whole" (or to live the "ultimate, *unorganized* life" in the mystical "trance state" that Gardner believed the artist attains in his highest moments) and the opposed condition of "imprisonment" by logic and the body imposed by the restrictions of time and space. In his outline, Gardner designates the desire for wholeness *A* and the time-space imprisonment *B*. Gardner then makes a list of the main characters and indicates their particular positions or ways of dealing with A and B.

Josef Mallin, an archcriminal (though he is elsewhere referred to as an "outraged philosopher-poet" [*KI*, 103]) beheaded some months earlier for crimes that were "the worst of the three main kinds of which the laws speak" (*KI*, 101), is an anarchist like those we have seen before. His characterization as a "nihilist, destroyer of churches, murderer of medical doctors" (*KI*, 92) links him specifically with the young bomber in "Pastoral Care" and mad Professor Hunter in "The Ravages of Spring." The three categories of crimes, Gardner's notes indicate, are based on the medieval (and ancient) notion of the tripartite soul (the concupiscent soul, the irascible soul, and the rational soul) and are what an earlier age classified as sins—respectively, sins of desire, sins of will, and sins of intellect. The most serious sins or crimes, of which Mallin is guilty, are those of the rational soul or intellect. Mallin's posture is to deny condition A, the desire for wholeness, and to hate condition B, the logical constraints of physicality, time, and space. The resultant frustration causes Mallin to attack and destroy the "illusions" of "the good state, art, religion, science" (Gardner Papers, box B-11). The narrator's father, a reliable voice in the story, as we shall see, neatly encapsulates Mallin's character and motives: "I'll tell you what it is with Josef Mallin. . . . He's convinced all ideals are a flight from reality. The unpleasant facts of life, he claims, charge the human soul with longing. They drive a man to make up a world that's better than ours. But that better world is mere illusion, says Mallin; and illusion, being false, a mere cowardly lie, is as foul as actuality. So he goes at the universe with dynamite sticks.—It's a natural mistake" (*KI*, 114). It is also a usual mistake in Gardner's fiction; all his nihilistic anarchists take this approach.

The narrator, Herr Vortrab, is the warden's deputy, who clings to the order of the "ancient regulations" and must improvise ways to run the prison, since the warden stays in his office and has not communicated with Vortrab or anyone else since Mallin's execution. According to Gardner's outline, the narrator "take[s] no stand" on condition A but "act[s] pragmatically to relieve the pain of B." His "guilt," which Gardner labels "mild" or "venial," derives from his "uncertainty about A." His actions are heroic in that he knows in advance that they are doomed to failure. He is thus better than Mallin, but he falls short of the true artist's ability to affirm both A and B—the ideal of aesthetic wholeness as well as what Gardner frequently called, in a phrase borrowed from William James, the "buzzing, blooming confusion" of the physical and temporal world.

The sympathetic Jewish guard Heller, Vortrab's only friend at the prison, has, Gardner notes, "Jewish answers" to the conflict. He affirms A, in spite of the apparent absurdity of doing so, and he acts essentially the same as Vortrab, sharing the same "guilt."

Vortrab's children, who seem rather normal in the glimpses we have of them at home, like their father "take no stand on A," but unlike their father they "do not act for others." They disobey, or obey reluctantly, refusing bedtime and coming to dinner only because they are hungry rather than because they are bidden to the table. Their guiding principle is the pursuit of pleasure, which makes them guilty of concupiscence, the less serious sins of desire. Gardner's note links the children's behavior and guilt with those of the "other prisoners" at the prison, not including the "old man," who is a special case.

The "old man," or "Professor" (as Heller calls him), is an elderly, emaciated—indeed, dying—prisoner to whom Heller introduces Vortrab. The professor was imprisoned long ago, unjustly, Heller is convinced, on charges that were never specified, and Heller is determined to try to have him released. The prisoner dies, however, before anything can be done, but not before he delivers a lecture on "Matter and Mind" to Heller and Vortrab. "There is no immateriality," he believes, only "gradations of matter of which man knows nothing," increasing in rarity until they reach the state of the "ultimate, unparticled matter" that "permeates" and "impels all things and thus *is* all things within itself. This matter is God." He further believes that pain and suffering in the "organic" life are a necessary preparation for the perfect blessedness of the "ultimate, unorganized life" to which death is merely a "painful metamorphosis" (*KI*, 96). Thus he affirms A (but only in a sort of hereafter), but, in what seems a masochistic perversion of affirmation, can affirm corporal life bound by logic, space, and time only by "enjoy[ing] suffering as prerequisite" (Gardner Papers, box B-11). Gardner's outline is ambiguous at this point, but it appears to classify the old man's position as a crime of irascibility, or sin of the will.

The worst of all the characters, it seems, is the absent or dead warden. Gardner's notes appear to attribute all three classes of crime to him, characterizing his position as one that will affirm A but "hate or feel indifferent to B." This character will "waste . . . life awaiting experience of A" until he comes to doubt and hate A as well as B. His guilt is "mortal" (Gardner Papers, box B-11). This meaning is substantiated in the story itself, when the narrator's father sums up the warden's position, much as he has done just previously with that of Mallin: "The Warden, now, he *believes* in the mystical experience. But, unfortunately, he's never had one. He wastes his life anticipating. It's a terrible crime. A mortal sin, I judge" (*KI*, 114).

Vortrab regards his aged father as senile and probably mad. The father, a member of Vortrab's household, combines the familiar Gardnerian figures of the true artist and the benignly "mad" or clownish affirmer of art and life. He is, in this story, the reliable voice of what Gardner himself affirms, as his penetrating analyses of Mallin and the warden show. He paints landscapes, and he is familiar with the "trance state" Gardner frequently cites as the apogee of the artist's experience. He knows, he says, "a little something of states of entrancement. Sometimes when you're painting, a kind of spell comes over you, and you know—you positively *know*—that there's no chance of erring with the picture at hand. You're nailed directly to the universe, and the same force that moves in the elm tree is moving your brush" (*KI*, 102). The note in Gardner's outline identifies the father as "the artist" who affirms both A and B, "moving between them."

The last character, Vortrab's wife, operates in a kind of perpetual "trance" state, somewhat ineffectually urging the children to eat supper, go to bed, and so forth, showing no particular concern when they ignore her to pursue their own concupiscent interests. According to Gardner's note on her character, she "misunderstand[s] both A & B, yet live[s] within both—less efficiently. (As a faulty parent, comforter, friend.)" She is apparently as guiltless, or almost so, as the father.

While the foregoing analysis of "The Warden" may seem strange to some, it is essentially the author's own "interpretation." It illustrates the extreme attention and "organization" Gardner lavished on his fiction, and I have no doubt that the same kind of detailed exposition is theoretically possible for all of Gardner's stories and novels.

Nevertheless, such an analysis does not begin to exhaust the multiple layers of meaning in a typical Gardner work. This story, for example, may also be read as a kind of religious allegory in which the absentee warden and his equally absent superiors in the Bureau of Justice may be seen as departed gods who have "abandoned" the prisonhouse world and universe. Vortrab, observing that in former times (before the "seat of government" was "so much farther away") the "chief justices themselves" sometimes visited the prison, clings to his belief that the warden is still "in there," pacing incessantly and refusing to communicate. Heller, however, listens at the door and hears no pacing, confirming his conclusion that "the Warden has abandoned us." Heller's practical observation is "Apparently it's all up to us, then"

(*KI*, 119). Numerous other details could be cited to support reading the story as a religious allegory, and it is entirely possible that other layers of allegory may be present as well.

Finally, there seems little hope for Vortrab's salvation, religious or otherwise. He grows inescapably toward assuming the warden's role, bringing new regulations, pardons, and death sentences in the name of the warden, who he knows has committed suicide. For Heller, there may be hope, though the matter is doubtful. He does not accept Vortrab's decrees happily, and Vortrab hears him pacing late at night (both of them have ceased going home in the evening), "occasionally pausing, deep in thought" (*KI*, 119). Even so, Heller's pacing is ominously reminiscent of the warden's.

"John Napper Sailing through the Universe"

The last story in book one of *The King's Indian*, "John Napper Sailing through the Universe," qualifies as fiction only marginally, if at all. John Napper, whom Gardner met at Southern Illinois University, was the artist who did the illustrations for Gardner's novel *The Sunlight Dialogues* (1972).[22] This "story" seems to be a largely factual account of a visit Gardner and his family paid to Napper and his wife while the Gardners were abroad in 1971.[23] Gardner does not even try to disguise the factual nature of events by altering the names of himself, his wife, and their children. They appear under their real names as John, Joan, Joel, and Lucy, as Napper and his wife, Pauline, appear under their own names. Undoubtedly, the reader has a strong sense that the events described actually happened, that this is not fiction in the usual sense, although no one would be likely to question it as fiction had Gardner changed the names of the characters. The questions that do arise here concern Gardner's intentions in writing such a piece and his decision to place it where he does in this collection.

Gardner may have had several intentions in writing this story. One, for example, may have been, as Cowart suggests, to do "for John Napper what Napper did for Lucy Gardner. As Napper had immortalized [Gardner's daughter] Lucy in a work of art, so Gardner will immortalize Napper" (Cowart, 89). Cowart also recognizes that Gardner had other, more important intentions, and quotes from the widely known Gardner interview with Marshall Harvey, in which Gardner identified this story as his "fundamental theory of art": "What Napper says is at the heart of it: an artist can't just describe the world, 'bitter reality'; the artist has to create new and wonderful possibilities" (Harvey, 81). Gardner might as easily and truly have said the same of "The Warden," "The Temptation of St Ivo," or any number of his other works, but certainly the John Napper story is largely an exemplification and dramatization of Gardner's "theory of art."

John Napper's life and career provided Gardner with a real-life example of an artist who had "gone to the pit" in his early paintings, seeking the "secret life" of the world and finding none: "He'd hounded light—not just visual light—straining . . . to get down to what was real, what was absolute; beauty not as someone else had seen it but beauty he could honestly find himself, and what he'd gotten was a picture of the coal pocket." That is, he had experienced the conflict dramatized in "The Warden," the contradiction between the ideal and the real. He had stared into the pit of existential nihilism. But unlike Josef Mallin or the Carbondale church bomber, John Napper had, "at the edge of self-destruction . . . I saw, jumped back. He would make up the world from scratch: Let there be light, a splendid garden. He would fabricate treasure maps. And he'd come to believe it" (*KI*, 133). Gardner, as narrator, is able to trace Napper's struggle and triumph by examining early paintings and comparing them with later ones. In Napper's Paris studio Gardner finds old paintings: "They were a shock: dark, furious, intellectual, full of scorn and something suicidal. Mostly black, with struggles of light, losing." Had Josef Mallin been a painter instead of an "outraged philosopher-poet," these are the paintings he would have done. Looking at these, Gardner finds it hard to understand why Napper "kept fighting instead of slitting his wrists" (*KI*, 124).

Later, in London, Gardner mentions the Paris paintings to Napper, who shows him even more terrible early paintings: "When he'd sorted out what he wanted us to see, we looked, heads touching, at the Napper retrospective. Ghoulish faces, fuliginous lump-people, terrible previews of Hiroshima, mournful cityscapes the texture of, roughly, dried blood. Here and there, there was a scraggly flower, a crushed bit of light" (*KI*, 125). Somehow, Napper penetrated the coal pocket and found on the other side the beauty, the light he could celebrate and affirm. His later paintings, the "big bright new ones," are full of light and flowers. Napper is the real-life analogue of Vortrab's father in "The Warden," the artist able to affirm both the ideal and the real.

Another of Gardner's motives in presenting this story as if it were autobiography or a personal essay rather than fiction was surely that he wished to demonstrate the close relationship between art and life. Life imitates art, Gardner frequently remarked, and that is why he insisted (most vehemently in his incendiary treatise *On Moral Fiction,*[24] but in fact he argued the point at every opportunity) that art must offer affirmative paradigms, models whose imitation will enhance and clarify life rather than debase and destroy it. It is as if he is saying in this story: Look, it doesn't just happen in my fiction; it happens in real life too, in the actual life of a man. Probably, he hoped the reader would notice that the only difference between this story and the more usual kind of fiction is in the names of the characters.

As far as the placement of "John Napper Sailing through the Universe" is concerned, I think that primarily it "had to do with light," as Gardner says of Napper's paintings. Both Cowart and Morris, in their analyses of *The King's Indian*, note that the "darkness" of "The Warden" is followed by the triumph of light in the John Napper story. In Gardner's scheme for the collection, we pass "midnight" in this story and move toward dawn in the section that follows, "Tales of Queen Louisa."

Tales of Queen Louisa

Book two of *The King's Indian*, the brief middle section entitled "Tales of Queen Louisa," comprises three "tales," averaging about fifteen pages each in length. The stories are "Queen Louisa," "King Gregor and the Fool," and "Muriel." They form an obvious unity, as if they were merely sections of a single longer story, and it therefore seems appropriate to consider them together. These are the least realistic of the stories in this collection, set in an unnamed medieval kingdom and imbued with a fairy-tale-like atmosphere. The normal restrictions of time, space, and logic (condition B of Gardner's notes on "The Warden") scarcely apply at all. Indeed, almost everything about these tales would suggest the world of children's fiction were it not for the intrusion of certain darker elements of experience: rape, adultery, out-of-wedlock pregnancy, and the shadow of a very real death that hovers in the background and is not made clear until the fourth "Queen Louisa" story, "Trumpeter," which appears in Gardner's later collection, *The Art of Living*.

Clearly, Gardner intended the Queen Louisa stories for an adult audience. He ran, it seems to me, a considerable risk of losing that audience's attention by presenting the stories in an Alice-in-Wonderland format. (More than one reviewer suggested Lewis Carroll as one of Gardner's sources.) The challenge Gardner thus posed for himself must have tested his skills as a writer of fiction as much as any of his realistic stories. When read with more than superficial attention, however, the stories have an almost irresistible charm that quickly draws the reader into the plot and encourages a Coleridgean suspension of disbelief in the fantastic elements. Approached from such a perspective, the plot itself becomes interesting and the reader actually comes to care about the characters, who are drawn with Gardner's characteristic sympathy and depth of insight into human nature and motivation. Moreover, the stories are texturally enriched by the author's broad and in many ways profound knowledge of the forms and conventions of medieval life and literature. The question remains, however, of what Gardner's larger intentions may have been.

Philosophically—and all Gardner's fiction has a philosophical dimension—it may be best to view these stories as parables or exempla, not unlike, for instance, Chaucer's Pardoner's exemplum of the three riotous young men who go in search of Death. In this light, the stories may be seen as Gardner's allegorical representation of the results of "making life art." That one should "make life art" is a familiar Gardnerian dictum that is more fully explored thematically in *The Art of Living*. Here, it may be, we have a preview of that theme.

"Mad Queen Louisa" (the opening phrase of the first story) is a central presence in all the stories, although the center of narrative interest is the former peasant girl who the queen decides is her "lost" daughter Muriel. It is a commonplace in Gardner criticism to observe that a kind of madness or lunacy, usually characterized as "benign" but perhaps better regarded as benevolent and beneficent, afflicts quite a number of Gardner's characters.[25] Queen Louisa is perhaps the only one of them who is "officially" mad, although some others come close—Peter Mickelsson, for example (the protagonist of the novel *Mickelsson's Ghosts*), is a survivor of at least one "nervous breakdown," and the narrator of "The Ravages of Spring," a medical doctor and veterinarian, it will be recalled, unofficially diagnoses Professor Hunter as mad. (Hunter's madness, however, is not of the benign sort.)

Although Queen Louisa's madness apparently has a dark origin—the reader infers that it was probably caused by the death of her daughter—its effects bring light and life wherever she goes. By her authority as queen and by clever manipulation of her gruff and irascible husband King Gregor and other characters, she imposes her own cheerfulness and good sense ultimately on the whole kingdom. Ironically, in spite of her delusions (or hallucinations) that she sometimes turns into a toad and was a lizard earlier in life, she becomes a model of a higher sanity that redeems both her family and her subjects.

In the first story, the queen decides that her pregnant, fourteen-year-old chambermaid is actually her long-lost daughter, the princess Muriel. King Gregor and his knights are supposedly away at the wars, and the chambermaid-daughter tells the queen that a witch has appeared on the mountain and routed the hermits from their cells. The queen summons the Royal Court and compels the justices to accompany her and Muriel to the mountain to confront the witch. At a remote monastery they find a "witchlike person," attended by an old red hound and a horde of wolves in monks' robes, trying to chop down a miraculously blooming rosebush, which grows larger and stronger with each stroke of the witch's ax.

In the confrontation that ensues, the witch defies Louisa's order to stop and spouts the usual doctrine of a Gardnerian nihilist: "'You see, my ancient enemy,' she cried, 'your whole life has been a terrible mistake! The forces of evil do exist! . . . We're cosmic accidents! . . . Life is gratuitous, it has no meaning till we make one up by our intensity'" (*KI*, 150–51). She goes on to say that she has "seduced" the queen's husband and filled him with her nihilistic doctrine. The queen puts an end to the charade by changing herself from the toad she has been into her "normal" self, "a magnificently beautiful redheaded woman" whose "white, white arms were so delicately dimpled at the elbows that neither knight nor wolf could refrain from licking his lips with desire."

Immediately the hound turns into King Gregor, the wolves turn into pious monks, and the witch becomes the queen's lady-in-waiting, Madame Logre. Gardner has in this scene reversed the usual method of allegory. Instead of presenting more or less realistic events that carry symbolic meaning, he has dramatized that meaning in fantastic events, leaving the reader to infer what "really" happened. Evidently, what has happened is a crisis in the royal marriage. Following the death of the original Muriel, King Gregor has slipped into an adulterous affair with Madame Logre. There are hints of psychological depth when the queen explains to her newfound daughter that her (Muriel's) "dramatic leaving gave your father ideas. The poor old fool was in his forties then, and, I'm sorry to say, all people in their thirties and early forties have this awful lust—this ridiculous hunger for experience, so to speak. And the pretty way you mocked him, of course, and flirted with him—" (*KI*, 152).

The queen's "madness" averts greater grief and restores a semblance of more normal order to the lives of all. They all, Madame Logre included, return to the palace, riding in a carriage driven by a coachman "who was silver-haired and wise" and beside whom sits a boy, his nephew. When the boy remarks that this is "a marvelous story to be in," the coachman replies with a wink, "You barely made it, laddie!" The coachman and the boy, besides representing a dramatic allusion to E. M. Forster's "The Celestial Omnibus" (another story about the power and importance of art), suggests a cameo appearance by the author himself. Gardner, silver-haired, is both coachman and narrator, and the boy may well be an actual nephew to whom he read or told this story.

The second of the Queen Louisa stories, "King Gregor and the Fool," begins, appropriately, as if it were a continuation: "Another thing that can be said about King Gregor is that he dearly loved his work" (*KI*, 153). The story is indeed a continuation, moving from the king's family problems dealt with in the preceding story to a consideration of one of his more important work problems. Gregor's royal work, which preoccupies him to the extent that he neglects his family, consists mainly of waging perpetual war against the neighboring and neighborly head of state, Just King John. As their armies clash bloodily on the fields below, Gregor and John direct their strategies and movements from twin mountains—as if they were, on one level, gods, or on another, chess players with real people for pieces.

When the armies break for lunch, John comes over to Gregor's mountain to visit. Gregor is in a gloomy mood, what with having to live with lunatics and being constantly bedeviled by his privileged fool, whose head he would like to chop off if only he could find a legitimate excuse. As they chat, two dukes arrive and present their respective kings with lists of the morning's dead and wounded. Gregor notices that John seems on the verge of tears (which he does not, however, shed), and a "mad, unheard-of question came drifting into King Gregor's mind but timidly fled before he was able to identify it" (*KI*, 156).

After the day's fighting goes badly for both sides, Gregor is assailed by "curious emotions and wordless intuitions, and one in particular, though for the life of him he couldn't make it come clear—some feeling of fundamental error, perhaps some error of his own, perhaps some error of all mankind" (*KI*, 158). His concentration is broken by intru-

35

sive visions of his wife, naked, and the thought never comes clear. The situation anticipates a similar scene in Gardner's later novel *Freddy's Book*, where another monarch, King Gustav of Sweden, actually achieves such an insight. As Gustav sits at his desk signing death warrants for enemies "real and imagined," he suddenly has a thought, "a vision which he scarcely understood and, in the heat of it, tore the parchment to shreds. 'Let the Riksdag decide,' he thought. 'What concerns all should have the approval of all.'"[26] Gustav's "vision," which is only slightly clearer to him than Gregor's is to Gregor, results (in Gardner's novel) in a major social change—the birth of democracy in the modern world.

King Gregor's question that will not come clear, the reader may infer, is, Why are we making war? and the "fundamental error" he senses but cannot identify is both his own and humankind's. It is the error of war. The distracting vision of his naked wife carries a subtext meaning that he should "make love, not war," but he is unable to make the connection. The intervention that will save Gregor's kingdom, and presumably John's, from endless and pointless slaughter must come from two certified lunatics, Queen Louisa and Gregor's fool. The queen visits the battlefield and is horrified to find the two armies charging murderously at each other. She yells "Stop!" and interrupts the proceedings, to the chagrin of the two kings, pointing out that "they could have *killed* each other!" Upon being informed by her husband that "That's the *idea*!" she delivers her judgment: "'Gregor,' she said, 'you people are all crazy'" (*KI*, 165).

In his rage at being forced by his "mad" wife to abandon the war, Gregor recalls that the fool has frequently recited this poem:

> *"You think I'm small because I'm lazy;*
> *But big brave knights get killed. That's crazy!"*

He concludes that the queen must have got her crazy ideas from the fool and decides to have him beheaded. When the fool claims that his "poem" is "from the Bible," Gregor calls for an expert on the Bible, and it happens that the only one "for miles around" is Just King John. Gregor summons John in the middle of the night to give his opinion on whether the fool's verses are actually from the Bible and therefore "not open to mere intellect's antilibrations, however insane one might privately think it." After some deliberation, John pronounces that "Yes! . . . The passage is distinctly Biblical. Loosely" (*KI*, 167–69).

The war, and war in general, is therefore over, and everyone rejoices. Thus a major ill of society is cured by the supposedly mad queen and her double, the fool.

Having solved her family problems (reacquiring her "lost" daughter or an acceptable substitute and reclaiming her errant husband) in the first story and eliminated war in the second, Queen Louisa in the third story, "Muriel," tackles the problems of social justice—poverty, exploitation, and inequality. In this story we learn of the Princess Muriel's background—her life before she went to the palace as a chambermaid and was discovered the next day by Queen Louisa to be her long-lost daughter. She had been a simple peasant girl, her parents "farming people" and her friends the children of tinkers, blacksmiths, and other farmers. The story begins by announcing that the "best thing about suddenly having been turned into a princess was that Muriel escaped all those tiresome and ultimately dangerous ideas that her friends imagined it was necessary to maintain" (*KI*, 171).

The "dangerous" ideas of her peasant friends, presumably, are revolutionary in nature. Indeed, the story is a parable of social revolution. Muriel's original peasant name was Tanya, a name with powerful contemporary revolutionary connotations. *Tania*, it will be recalled, is the "revolutionary" name Patricia Hearst was given during the period of her abduction by the Symbionese Liberation Army. Gardner adapts the Patricia Hearst story in Muriel's account of her having been abducted (twice—once before her elevation to royalty and again afterward) by the notorious anarchist, rapist, and murderer Vrokror. She comes to sympathize with her captor, to the extent that she is carrying his child.

When she is abducted the second time, after bouncing out of the royal coach in a forest, she awakens from her faint in the company of all her old peasant friends, who turn out to be in league with Vrokror. The anarchist, bent on destroying all governments, starting with King Gregor's, plans, regretfully, to use Muriel as a hostage to lure the queen to him. He will then murder the queen, thus undermining morale in the kingdom. (His designs recall Morgan le Fay's plot in *Sir Gawain and the Green Knight* to undermine Arthur's kingdom by frightening Guinevere to death.) Muriel inserts a coded message into Vrokror's letter to the queen, and Gregor arrives with his knights to rescue Muriel and rout the revolutionaries. Vrokror escapes, and the queen arrives to proclaim all the injured peasants her long-lost children, princes and princesses. Louisa blames the problems on "tiresome and ultimately dangerous ideas" (ironically echoing the earlier description of the revolutionary ideas of Muriel's friends) and whips with a willow switch all those guilty, including Madame Logre, whose protestation that she "never did a thing" convicts her of what Louisa calls "the most tiresome and ultimately dangerous idea of all." Only Gregor and Muriel escape switching, and they all, including Muriel's former peasant friends, return to the palace to live as royalty. The queen pronounces what appears to be the message of the story: "All error," she says, "begins with soreheads" (*KI*, 192–94).

The "Tales of Queen Louisa" thus embody in their fanciful trappings serious commentary on individual, social, and political realities. The solutions to problems at all levels of society, Gardner suggests, are to be found in the values of love and community. Muriel believes that Queen Louisa is "a kind of saint" (*KI*, 181), and in the terms of Gardner's fiction, so she is. Her "madness" represents the kind of higher sanity that can transmute the dreary and disappointing world of ordinary reality into the beauty of aesthetic wholeness. That is to say, her achievements represent the power of art.

"The King's Indian"

When asked what were his own favorites among his works, the ones he thought were best, Gardner would often cite the novella (or "tale") "The King's Indian" and the epic poem *Jason and Medeia*. Early reviewers overwhelmingly contradicted the author's estimate of his epic (quite wrongheadedly, later critical studies have argued) but by almost as wide a margin supported his high opinion of the novella. Indeed, Gardner was writing both works at about the same time, in 1971 (Howell, 1980, xviii), and there are certain affinities between them.

For one thing, both the epic and the tale make extensive use of earlier works of other authors as "sources," and for another, a number of the unusual, even bizarre words (some of them never elsewhere used in English or any other language) that bristle from the pages of *Jason and Medeia* also appear in "The King's Indian"—such words as *flambuginous, pancrastical, quisquos* (*sic;* in *Jason and Medeia* it is spelled *quisquous*), and *zacotic*, to name a few.[27] Regardless of its ultimate merit, "The King's Indian" is certainly among the most intricately and cleverly constructed works of fiction one is likely to encounter.

Another work Gardner had recently completed when he was writing "The King's Indian" was the large and complex novel *The Sunlight Dialogues* (1972), which also shows an interesting affinity with the shorter work. The novel opens with a scene very possibly located in some afterlife, with three persons present: former police chief Clumly (the protagonist of the novel), the "oldest Judge in the world," and a male nurse who is the judge's attendant. Clumly has visited the judge and the two drink whisky, talking of old times. The obviously symbolic scene suggests the Christian Trinity of Father, Son, and Holy Ghost. The judge remarks to his attendant after Clumly leaves, "I made that man. I created him, you might say. I created them all." A moment later he says to the attendant, "You're like a son to me," and the attendant replies, "As to that . . . I'm what I am," echoing Jehovah's cryptic identification of Himself to Moses. Clumly, the other member of the trio, is represented in John Napper's frontispiece illustration of the scene as a pure white silhouette, and the narrator notes a division of opinion in Batavia over whether Clumly had "gone away somewhere or died," both of which circumstances suggest a ghostly status.[28] Most prominent among the scene's literary ancestors is the "Prologue in Heaven" to Goethe's *Faust*.

Similarly, "The King's Indian" begins with an apparently "heavenly" scene involving three persons: the "ancient mariner" who will serve as the secondary narrator, a "guest" who will be his principal audience, and an attendant angel who will keep them supplied with "spirits." This celestial tavern scene actually provides the narrative framework of the tale, reappearing several times during the course of the story. With this framework, Gardner follows the narrative technique of several models, serving himself as primary narrator but assigning most of the narration to the "old loon." This is Chaucer's method in the *Canterbury Tales*, as it is also that of Coleridge in *The Rime of the Ancient Mariner*, a closer model. A third model is Conrad's "Youth" (another classic sea tale that must be accounted among Gardner's sources), in which "Marlow" serves as a secondary narrator—also to an audience sitting around a table drinking—of events that happened many years before.

Like much if not all of Gardner's fiction, "The King's Indian" operates simultaneously on multiple levels of meaning, a fact that is ironically underscored by the secondary narrator's (the aged and/or deceased Jonathan Upchurch) occasional protestations to the contrary. He introduces his tale with an admonition to the guest to "understand from the outset it has no purpose to it, no shape or form or discipline but the tucket and boom of its highflown language and whatever dim flickers that noise stirs up in yer cerebrium, sir—." The reader immediately has cause to doubt the disclaimer when Jonathan goes on to say that he will speak "of such matters as devils and angels and the making of man, which is my subject, sir" (*KI*, 197). In a later interlude, section X, in which the framework scene reappears with the guest's objection that he has never heard a more outrageous yarn, the mariner himself suggests the presence of deeper levels of meaning: "'There's truths and truths,' says he, full of thunder. 'If a narrative don't seem to make much sense, mine deeper—that's the ticket!'" The guest is not yet sadder and wiser—"A straw for yer levels!" he snorts scornfully—but he is inescapably hooked by the tale: "Tell on!" he urges (*KI*, 235–36).

Cowart, in a masterly analysis excerpted in part 3 of this book, exposes in detail the national and political level of allegory in "The King's Indian," showing how the characters and events in the story reflect the progress of the American "ship of state," from its theoretical and idealistic origins through its history of trial and compromise and on to its possible future. As Cowart also suggests, the story operates on philosophical and aesthetic planes as well. The youthful Jonathan Upchurch (age nineteen, just a year younger than Conrad's Marlow in "Youth") finds himself embarked on what Conrad calls one of those "voyages that seem ordered for the illustration of life, that might stand for a symbol of existence." His maturation, his initiation into life and philosophy, thus become part of the great tradition of sea stories that goes back to antiquity, to the voyages of Odysseus and Jason.

During the course of his voyage on the whaler *Jerusalem*, Jonathan must penetrate layer upon layer of false "presentation" in his search for the heart of meaning, the "truth" not only about the ship he is on and its mysterious population and purposes, but about the nature of existence itself. He is faced with various philosophical alternatives, the most dangerous of which (as always in Gardner's fiction) is the lure of nihilistic existentialism. He "teeters on the rim" of the abyss both philosophically—when subjected to demoralizing events and to the arguments of characters like Wolff and Wilkins—and literally, when high in the ship's rigging he almost takes a fatal "step to Nowhere." His friend Billy More saves him from that fate and urges him to "Keep yer bearings, that's the secret. . . . Know in the back of yer mind where ye stand, whatever ye happen to think of the place, and banish all thought of Nowhere by keeping yer mind from belief in it. . . . If ye *must* think, think of Faith itself. . . . Faith, that's the secret! Absolute faith like a seagull's" (*KI*, 238). The strategy works literally, as far as climbing in the rigging is concerned, and the allegorical implication is only thinly veiled: resisting the temptation to believe in the nihilist's meaninglessness also involves an act of willful faith.

On the aesthetic level, Jonathan proves to be almost as adroit a maker of fictions as his creator. His imaginative and contradictory stories about his background show real talent and qualify him as a figure of the "good artist." (His fictions are always affirmative and life enhancing, directed to moral ends, not debasing and degrading.) On the other side, the maniacal magician Dr. Luther Flint represents the "bad artist" whose tricks and illusions serve only himself and impoverish the lives of everyone around him. Flint's Ahab-like obsession, his "grand purpose," requires that he achieve either "Death or Absolute Vision among the Vanishing Isles." He snatches after godhood in the name of self, not unlike Professor Hunter in "The Ravages of Spring," and when he fails (and when he is outsmarted by the better artist, Jonathan, in a chess game that Jonathan opens with the legendary move "the king's Indian"), he dies. Flint's death is even more spectacular than Hunter's being carried away by four tornadoes: spontaneous combustion. In both cases a "bad artist" has offended nature, has committed hubris, and nature destroys them.

Jonathan comes through his experience profoundly wiser. He has learned the Gardnerian lesson of the necessity of human community and love in a "changeable" universe where there are "no stable principles." He hails the remnants of the ship's population, his "fellow Cains," as "you orphans, you bandy-legged, potbellied, pig-brained, belly-dancing killers of the innocent whale! Eyes forward, you niggers, you Chinese Irish Mandalay Jews, you Anglo-Saxons with jackals' eyes. We may be the slime of the earth but we've got our affinities! On to Illinois the Changeable!"—as angelic seabirds circle, crying "*Tekeli-li! Tekeli-li!*" (the mysterious cry of the seabirds in Poe's *Narrative of Arthur Gordon Pym*) in echo to his command to "tack alee." The Holy Ghost, "disguised as a sea-boobie sitting by my shoulder," confirms the command, "Tack alee!" and returns Jonathan's advice to "hang on" (*KI*, 323). The advice to "tack alee and hang on" could well serve as a metaphoric representation of the message Gardner inculcates in all his fiction.

"Tacking alee," turning to go with the wind, also recalls the Sunlight Man's explanation of divination: "Divination is man's attempt to find out what the universe is doing. Magic is man's ridiculous attempt to make the gods behave as mortals. After divination one acts *with* the gods. You discover which way things are flowing, and you swim in the same direction" (*SD*, 419). Unwittingly, Jonathan has practiced divination and can now flow with the universe; Flint, though he "hunted all his life for some holiness past magic" (*KI*, 308), never rises beyond the attempt to compel the universe and is therefore swept away.

The matter of Gardner's sources and his use of them lies close to the heart of his technique as a writer of fiction. More than perhaps any other modern writer of comparable note, Gardner borrowed plots, characters, scenes, words, phrases, sentences, and passages from other writers—ancient, medieval and modern—and converted them to his own use, often embellishing them or changing them and always integrating them with his own work so that they seem like organic parts of it. "I use everything," Gardner would frequently respond when asked about his sources, and so he did. "The King's Indian" is an especially notable example of this practice.

Both Morris and Cowart document Gardner's borrowings from Poe, Melville, and Mark Twain. Much of the plot, both in its broad outline and in many passages and details, derives from Poe's *Narrative of Arthur Gordon Pym*, and several plot elements and characters, as well as several phrases and longer passages, come from Melville's *Moby-Dick* and his poem "Clarel." Melville's "Billy Budd" also supplies part of the inspiration for at least one character, that of Billy More, though Cowart cites Gardner's original intention to name this character Tom More and notes the double significance of the reference to the author of *Utopia* (which means "nowhere" and thus connects with the fatal "step" Billy saves Jonathan from taking) (Cowart, 109, 209). Most obviously, Coleridge's *Rime of the Ancient Mariner* provides the characters of the aged Jonathan-as-narrator and the initially unwilling guest-as-audience, as well as the narrative framework for the tale, and the resolution to the story's plot comes when Augusta (Miranda) "blesses [Jonathan] unaware" (*KI*, 322), as Coleridge's mariner initiates the resolution of his predicament by blessing the water snakes "unaware." Gardner even imitates the form of Coleridge's "marginal gloss" by placing the notation in the margin. There are also elements from Poe's "Ligeia," which Jonathan cites by name (*KI*, 310), and the black harpooner James Ngugi, noble and generous, is in some sense a reincarnation of Mark Twain's Nigger Jim.

Yet another influence, as noted earlier, is Conrad's sea story "Youth," which employs a similar framework and setting and offers a parallel in the allegorical name of its ship: the *Judea*. Interestingly, Conrad's story mentions a ship named the *Miranda* (or *Melissa*), and the cause of the fire in the *Judea's* cargo that ultimately destroys the ship is said to be "spontaneous combustion." Of course, the more obvious source of the name *Miranda* and of the relationship between the magician-father and his daughter is Shakespeare's play *The Tempest,* and there are, as Gardner remarks in one of his authorial intrusions, thinking no doubt of the instances in Dickens's *Bleak House* and Charles Brockden Brown's *Wieland*, literary antecedents for the death of a character by spontaneous combustion.

This does not discount, however, the fact that Gardner's borrowings and allusions often reflect more than one source at the same time, as we saw earlier in the case of the character Billy More. In the same authorial intrusion just mentioned, Gardner identifies himself by name as "the man that, with the help of Poe and Melville and many another man, wrote this book," and describes the book as "not a toy but a queer, cranky monument, a collage: a celebration of all literature and life; an environmental sculpture, a funeral crypt" (*KI,* 316). Thus the texture of Gardner's narrative is not a result of merely stringing together a number of discrete sources but a much richer, more tightly woven blend of multiple connections into a single, seamless fabric.

The Children's Stories

As Gardner acknowledged in an interview with Roni Natov and Geraldine DeLuca (excerpted in part 2),[29] his interest in writing for children developed from his practice of presenting his own children, each Christmas, with a story he had written. This interest eventually led to his publishing five books for children in a three-year period, including three collections of four stories each (*Dragon, Dragon and Other Tales* [1975], *Gudgekin the Thistle Girl and Other Tales* [1976], and *The King of the Hummingbirds and Other Tales* [1977]); a collection of humorous poems about animals, entitled *A Child's Bestiary* (1977); and the children's novel *In the Suicide Mountains* (1977).

All the children's books were met with mixed but predominantly favorable reviews that most frequently cited their wit, irony, felicity of language, zaniness, and gently inculcated morality as virtues. The minority of reviewers who disliked the books most often complained that the level of philosophical abstraction in some of the stories and poems exceeded the comprehension of children and seemed more appropriate for an adult audience. Some also objected to the irreverent liberties Gardner took with standard fairy-tale themes and situations.[30]

Later, more measured critical responses generally reflect the reviewers' initial assessments. Cowart devotes a chapter of his study of Gardner's fiction, *Arches and Light*, to the children's books and finds them almost entirely laudable. In his perceptive and informed analyses of individual stories, Cowart demonstrates that the children's stories embody many of the same themes and concerns as Gardner's adult fiction and that while they are here keyed to the understanding of young or adolescent readers, adults may also find entertainment in these stories. DeLuca and Natov, in one of the very few critical essays devoted to the children's books, take a more balanced view, praising them for their virtues but branding them all as "partial failures," chiefly because "the sophisticated humor and psychological insights of his most successful stories suggest that they might really fare best with adults."[31]

It seems to me that the objection of inappropriateness to younger readers is not entirely justified, at least as it applies to the three collections of stories. Gardner made it clear in the interview with Natov and DeLuca that he was writing for what he thought of as a fairly sophisticated young audience. Speaking of "The Griffin and the Wise Old Philosopher," he said, "It's for older kids," and went on to say that the same is "true of most of my fairy tales. All of them, in fact, with the possible exception of *Dragon, Dragon,* I really meant for kids who have been through fairy tales and are ready for slight variety" (119). Moreover, it is true of all Gardner's fiction that the author deliberately sought to make his work appealing on a variety of levels, from the popular to the most intellectually sophisticated.[32] The same principle obviously applies to the children's stories. While they possess ample humor of the absurdly incongruous type and plot lines simple enough to appeal to younger children, they are also filled with pearls of wit, irony and "philosophical abstraction" suited for precocious, older, or even adult readers. The stories therefore have a breadth of appeal rather than a narrowness. If this is a flaw, we may nevertheless be confident that it was intentionally designed by the author.

Dragon, Dragon and Other Tales

The title story of *Dragon, Dragon* exhibits features common to all or most of the stories in all three collections. These elements include a setting in an unnamed and completely anachronistic kingdom that can only be called fairyland, a place in which ideas, objects, and characters from the distant past mingle freely with those from more modern times. Other common features include some crisis or danger that threatens to reduce the kingdom to disorder or chaos; a reward of half the kingdom and the hand of the princess in marriage to whoever can solve the problem; and the solution of the problem by some unlikely hero—the unpromising third son of some tradesman, a girl chimney sweep, a thistle girl, a miller, a tailor, or, in one case, a "wise old philosopher." Naturally, all the stories have a moral dimension. As Gardner said in the interview with Natov and DeLuca, "every tale presents some basic idea of how to live with other people" in a world "in which you're not really sure of what's going on" (Natov and DeLuca, 119).

In "Dragon, Dragon" the kingdom is plagued by the monthly depredations of a dragon that evidently takes considerable delight in disorder. Every full moon the dragon emerges from his lair and perpetrates such horrors as frightening maidens, stopping up chimneys, breaking store windows, setting clocks back, making dogs bark "until no one could hear himself think," tipping over fences, robbing graves, putting frogs in drinking water, tearing the last chapters out of novels, changing house numbers "so that people crawled into bed with their neighbors' wives," stealing spark plugs out of cars, putting firecrackers in people's cigars, stealing clappers from church bells, springing all the bear traps, and, ultimately, "chang[ing] around all the roads in the kingdom so that people could not get anywhere except by starting out in the wrong direction" (*DD*, 3–4). Something for everyone.

The king's knights, being cowardly, are useless against this menace, and the wizard, elderly and forgetful, has lost his book of spells. In desperation, the king makes the standard offer—half the kingdom and the hand of the princess—"to anyone who can make the dragon stop."

A "wise old cobbler" considers the king's offer and rejects it, since he's already married and thinks half the kingdom would be "too much responsibility." The cobbler's three sons, however, think the game worth the candle and resolve, one at a time, to tackle the problem. The eldest, distinguished by his cleverness and "known far and wide for how quickly he could multiply fractions in his head," goes first, confident that he can slay the dragon by cunning. He seeks his father's advice only out of politeness, and when that advice turns out to be that he should recite the following poem, "Dragon, dragon, how do you do? / I've come from the king to murder you," the son rejects it as stupid, even though his father assures him that if he will "say it very loudly and firmly . . . the dragon will fall, God willing, at your feet" (*DD*, 9). The son approaches the dragon's lair disguised as a brush salesman and is, of course, devoured.

The middle son is very strong, famed for his ability to lift up the corner of a church. As he sets out, his father repeats his advice, which this son also rejects, opting for a direct physical attack. The dragon hides above his door, so that the son charges under him, slamming into the wall and knocking himself unconscious. The dragon devours this son in more leisurely fashion, storing his horse in the freezer to eat later.

The cobbler's youngest son is neither clever nor strong, and he has serious misgivings about this whole business. He does, however, possess certain less flamboyant virtues: he is decent and honest, and always minds his elders. And so it happens that he takes his father's advice and recites the poem when confronted by the dragon. The boy is scarcely able to walk in his oversize suit of armor, and he can lift only one end of his heavy sword. The dragon is reduced to helpless, tearful laughter by the absurdity of the situation and falls on his back at the boy's feet. The boy is moved to righteous indignation by the dragon's ridicule of both his mission and his father's poem, and he manages to stand the sword on its hilt and let it fall on the dragon's neck. The dragon is beheaded, the other sons crawl gratefully out of his innards, and the three brothers claim the treasures from the dragon's cave, among which is the wizard's lost book of spells. Later, the youngest son claims his other rewards.

The obvious moral here is that decency, honesty, and respect for one's elders may be better weapons against the threat of disorder than either arrogant cunning or mindless strength. These virtues alone, however, do not fully account for the third son's victory. He finds the strength and the intelligence to kill the dragon only after the dragon's ridicule of everything he values moves him first to annoyance, then to anger, and finally to a "terrific rage." The dragon, like all Gardner's dragons, is a nihilist, a spokesman against all sense of purpose, value, meaning, or mission, and we are to understand that the young man's wrath is righteous and appropriate when directed against such an object. Behind this, I suspect, we can hear also a notable dictum of William Blake, whom Gardner greatly admired, to the effect that "the voice of honest indignation is the voice of God."

In "The Tailor and the Giant" the crisis that afflicts the kingdom is equally frequent and, physically, more dangerous. A giant comes out on the first Monday of each month and eats everything he can catch—horses, cows, and ministers first, and he has begun on the schoolteachers. Fear that the giant may graduate to more important morsels once the schoolteachers are exhausted moves the king to raise an army by conscription: every man must serve for thirty days in the royal army.

A tailor, so timid that he rarely leaves his shop for fear of being bitten by a dog, beaten by young cutthroats, or brained by a flowerpot falling from a second-story window, is terrified at the prospect of being drafted and resolves to demonstrate against the draft. He makes signs saying Love in big red letters but is unable to carry out his protest for fear his neighbors might laugh at him, the king might be cross, or the signs might attract the giant's attention and get him eaten.

When the giant finds the tailor in his shop and bends down to extract him, the king and the thirty-day army happen along. The king flees down an alley, exhorting his army, "Charge, brave boys!" The army, "being mostly young and foolish," charges, and although its members fight gallantly, the giant scoops them all up and carries them home, presumably to eat. The tailor is moved by the army's gallantry and unhappy at his own cowardice, and when the king passes a new law requiring the remaining men in the kingdom to serve for ninety days in the royal army, he resolves to support the effort by demonstrating with signs that read "JOIN NOW!" in big red letters. Again he is unable to carry out his plan because of his fear.

The giant returns and reaches into the shop for the tailor, just as the king and the new ninety-day army, "even more gallant, being younger and less experienced," happen by. The same result ensues, and the tailor sinks deeper into gloom as he realizes that the armies have been lost to protect his "worthless life." At last, despite his fears, he leaves his shop in the night "to meet the doom he so richly deserved." To his surprise, nothing happens to him as he walks to the city limits. No dogs bite him, and no cutthroats attack, although once he hears, ominously, "a kind of noise like a pot breaking, falling from a second-story window a block away" (*DD*, 29).

As the tailor walks into the woods, the giant spots him from the second-story window of his castle and sends first his dogs and then his cutthroats to capture the tailor, who is oblivious to his pursuers in his preoccupation with a more compelling anxiety: he is trying to reason out his guilt and responsibility for the loss of the armies, wrestling with the question of whether he deserves his fate. The dogs and cutthroats overrun him and are lost in the quicksand, prompting the giant himself to come after him. Still preoccupied, the tailor watches the giant follow the dogs and cutthroats into the quicksand and "sink out of sight, flailing his arms and yelling 'Zounds!'" (*DD*, 33).

At this point, the tailor realizes that he cannot determine the degree of his guilt until he knows whether the armies have actually been eaten. He goes to the castle, finds them alive in the dungeon, and releases them. They had been too lean to eat, from their military training, and too small as well, since, "being young, they weren't any of them more than half-grown." They are able to escape without fear of pursuit by the giant's wife, because she is a hopeless coward, "afraid of everything—dogs, young cutthroats, flowerpots dropping from second-story windows" (*DD*, 35).

As they all return triumphantly home, the tailor speaks "earnestly of the lesson he'd learned, how fear is all in the mind, really—though cutthroats are a serious business, of course, and there are, of course, some dogs that would as soon bite you as look at you, and flowerpots *do* sometimes fall into the street, endangering the casual passerby." The tailor notices that the soldiers who are his companions are hurrying through the dark places, "glancing apprehensively" at every shadow, and "listening as if with hearts stopped whenever they heard the whirr of something falling" (*DD*, 35).

The lessons the tailor learns go beyond the insight that fear is "all in the mind." More importantly, he (and the young reader, if the story is successful) learns a lesson in commonality: that we are all subject to the same kinds of fears and that while there is some basis for being prudent around vicious dogs, cutthroats, and second-story windows, it is foolish and life denying to be so overruled by fear that one cannot participate meaningfully in life. There is also a lesson, of course, about the irrationality of war in the repeated implication that wars are conducted by cowardly adults who use inexperienced (and therefore "gallant") children as cannon fodder. And finally, there is a lesson about not taking unnecessary risks when the tailor, rewarded with the princess's hand in marriage, lives with her "happily ever after in the royal palace, never leaving it for anything, not even to go get the mail" (*DD*, 35.)

The third story in *Dragon, Dragon*, "The Miller's Mule," possesses a psychological complexity that is likely to challenge the understanding of adult readers, let alone children. Yet the story line, as Cowart observes, is sufficiently humorous to hold the reader's attention, although he remarks that the story "seems to deploy its standard fairy-tale features—the three hazards, the helpful counselor, the winning of riches and a princess—to no particular end" (Cowart, 132).

"The Miller's Mule" is actually an allegory—of mythic import—concerning enmity, forbearance, and reconciliation and repentance, although these operations are fully understood by only one character, the mule. It would be unrealistic to imagine that a young reader could intellectually understand the way the story works, and surely the author labored under no such illusion. He hoped, rather, that the story would erect in the reader's mind a mythic paradigm with which the reader could perhaps later integrate certain archetypal human experiences.

The miller decides to shoot his mule, which has grown too old to work, but is dissuaded by the mule's pleas and by his offer to make the miller a wealthy man. The decisive factor in the miller's sparing the mule, however, seems to be that he is "basically a kindly person." The mule, on the other hand, is "actually a wicked and spiteful creature" and besides that has a plan to get the miller killed.

The mule will make his master wealthy if they go before the king and the miller will agree with everything the mule says. The mule then executes three increasingly complex stratagems designed to have the miller executed for treason: he claims that his master can turn boulders into rubies; that he can make the rivers of the kingdom run backward, turning the kingdom into a desert; and that he can overthrow all the kings "from here to Latvia." Each of the mule's murderous plans is thwarted by a person with one brown eye and one blue eye—an old woman who waves her walking stick over the boulders and turns them into rubies, a hunchbacked old friar who reverses the river with a wave of his stick, and finally the princess, who with a wave of her ivory comb causes the earth to open and swallow the neighboring kings. As each plot fails, the miller threatens again to shoot his mule for attempting to murder him, but each time the mule claims that he foresaw it all. Each time, the miller relents, not because he is convinced the beast is telling the truth but because he is uncertain about what the truth is. After the third plot fails, the miller holds his pistol to the mule's head for a long time but at last "threw down the pistol and stamped his foot. 'Confound it,' he said 'a person just can't tell.'" The miller, who has married the witch-princess, allows the mule to live with them in the palace. The mule never tries to kill his master again, partly in his own self-interest, and over the years becomes more friendly. When he dies, the mule leaves all he has to the miller, along with "a note so touching that the miller could not help but weep" (*DD*, 54).

The miller's uncertainty about the mule's intentions reflects the uncertainty Gardner cited in the Natov-DeLuca interview as a major theme of all his children's stories, and the miller's forbearance—his refusal to execute the mule on uncertain evidence—presents one "basic idea of how to live with other people" in a world where people's motives and the precise natures of situations are often necessarily uncertain. Moreover, the mule had evidently been the miller's deadly enemy but was eventually reconciled and converted to an attitude of love and respect by virtue of his master's forbearance, compassion, and unwillingness to resort to an extreme remedy.

The final story in *Dragon, Dragon*, "The Last Piece of Light," affords Gardner the opportunity to work with two of his favorite symbolisms, darkness and light. As usual, darkness represents evil, hopelessness, disorder, and denial of life, and light represents hope, vitality, and affirmation.

The problem is that a "withered old man with one glass eye" is stealing all the light in the world so that everyone except him and his one friend, a "cruel old 'mizer'" of Utrecht (both of whom have long since given up the habit of eating), will starve to death and he will be "Master of the World." The heroine, a "chimney-girl by the name of Chimorra" who lives with a "cruel lady boardinghouse-keeper" and spends most of her time happily dusting soot off bricks in dark flues, overhears the plot. On the advice of "the Lady of the North Star," who appears to Chimorra in a dream, she steals (or "borrows") a single sliver of light from the last load the withered old man brings in and hides it in her locket. The Lady of the North Star also teaches Chimorra a poem to recite if she ever becomes depressed and needs help.

Next morning, all the light is gone; "the whole world was as dark as a pit, and all the people were moaning and sighing, horribly depressed" (*DD*, 64). Chimorra foolishly reveals to the boardinghouse lady that she has preserved a piece of light in her locket; as a result, she must flee to the forest to escape the old woman's attempts to steal it from her. In the forest she meets the prince, who is lost, and offers to try to guide him back to the palace. She is unable to remember the poem she is supposed to recite in a situation like this, and she becomes separated from the prince when the one-eyed man, who has learned that she has a piece of light, impersonates the Lady of the North Star and lures her away. Chimorra leaves her locket with the prince, who eventually finds his way back to the palace "by pure luck."

Chimorra is enslaved by the one-eyed man and the mizer for many years, and the kingdom languishes in darkness, the people "growing colder and weaker from hunger every hour" and slipping into an even more terrible "spiritual gloom" (*DD*, 71). One "night"—"the coldest night in the world"—Chimorra overhears the mizer complaining about his inability to "*count* properly in this confounded gloom," and the word *gloom* triggers her memory of the poem, which she promptly recites:

> *"Gloom is here, gloom is there,*
> *But I am the North Star's friend."*

With the magic words of the poem, the Lady of the North Star is "freed" to go to the prince and whisper in his ear, "Open up the locket, stupid. What do you think she gave it to you for?" (*DD*, 72). He opens the locket, and the light bursts out, growing by reflection in the mirror, the jewels in his crown, and the chandelier, and fills the world, triggering a great celebration. Chimorra and the prince are reunited and proceed to become acquainted in the daylight, as the one-eyed man and the mizer stand behind the door, shaking their heads in disgust.

While the symbolism of light and darkness is obvious enough, the crisis in the story suggests wider implications—of worldwide calamity and the threat of ecological disaster. And while one cannot be certain that Gardner intended such a reference, since the matter had not been brought to popular attention when he wrote the story, the description of the effects of darkness on the world inevitably must suggest (to an adult reader in the 1990s, at least) the predicted horrors of "nuclear winter."

Gudgekin the Thistle Girl and Other Tales

The title story in this collection borrows extensively from Cinderella, as, to a less extent, did "The Last Piece of Light." Like Chimorra in the earlier tale, the heroine, Gudgekin, is forced by a wicked guardian—in this case a stepmother—to work slavishly at a lowly occupation. Although the use to which people put thistles "in those days" is no longer known, the narrator says, Gudgekin must work seven days a week to gather ever-increasing quantities of the prickly plants, under threat of being sent to the Children's Home. Despite her hard life, Gudgekin remains cheerful about her own condition and feels sorrow only for the misery of others.

When Gudgekin becomes acquainted with the queen of the fairies, the queen is impressed by her compassionate nature (which she seems to recognize as too compassionate for Gudgekin's own good) and befriends her, having the fairies gather thistles for her while the queen arranges Gudgekin's introduction to high society. She provides Gudgekin with spendid clothing and conveys her in a flying chariot to the kingdom's royal ball, where Gudgekin meets and charms the prince, known for his subtlety and shrewdness. The next day Gudgekin attends the royal fox hunt, where the prince is further entranced, and the day after that, a Sunday, she attends church, followed by the royal picnic and dancing beside the river.

As they dance, the prince asks Gudgekin her name. When she tells him that her name is Gudgekin and she is a thistle girl, he refuses to believe her and thinks she is teasing. Gudgekin interprets this behavior as ridicule and runs off weeping, deeply offended.

Numerous complications ensue: the prince advertises for information on Gudgekin; the stepmother hears of this action and sends Gudgekin to the Children's Home under a spell, then disguises herself as Gudgekin and reports to the prince; when the prince asks her to demonstrate her remarkable thistle-gathering skills, the stepmother fails and retrieves Gudgekin from the Home for help; Gudgekin is much changed, however, and will not help her, which enables the shrewd prince to see through the stepmother's trick; and the prince again advertises for Gudgekin to forgive him and come to the palace. Gudgekin, who now values her self-respect above all things, remains offended and is determined to have nothing to do with the prince.

The solution is brought about by a situation that will reappear in Gardner's later story "Vlemk the Box-Painter." Word goes out that the prince has fallen ill and is near death from sorrow. The fairy queen feels responsible and falls ill herself, threatening the lives of all the fairies, who, if the queen dies, will also die out of sympathy. She tells Gudgekin that the only thing that can possibly save her is Gudgekin's accompanying her to visit the prince. At first Gudgekin refuses, but she relents for the sake of the fairies.

They visit the prince, who indeed appears to be on his deathbed. "Woe is me," he explains to Gudgekin. "I was once that proud, shrewd prince you know, and this is what's become of me. For I hurt the feelings of the beautiful Gudgekin, whom I've given my heart and who refuses to forgive me for my insult, such is her pride and uncommon self-respect" (*G*, 19).

Gudgekin's wounded pride evaporates at this revelation, and she tearfully berates herself for her misguided self-regard: "You have given your heart to a fool . . . simple-minded as a bird! First I had pity for everyone but myself, and then I had pity for no one but myself, and now I pity all of us in this miserable world, but I see by the whiteness of your cheeks that I've learned too late!" (*G*, 19).

Pressing his advantage, the prince extracts from her an irrevocable promise of love and forgiveness forever. When she promises, rashly, he leaps out of bed, removes the ghastly makeup from his face, and dances Gudgekin around the room. Although she tries briefly to be offended by the trick, she at last capitulates and apparently accepts the prince's stated intention to "watch out for witches and live happily ever after."

In the Natov-DeLuca interview, Gardner characterized Gudgekin's switch from caring only about others to caring only about herself as a retreat into nihilism. It was no doubt inevitable that nihilism would appear as a threat to a character's psychic well-being even in the children's stories, though it is here disguised as mere selfish concern, as if Gardner's intention were to show the maladaptive nature of such selfishness and thereby nip in the bud a trait that may lead to full-blown nihilism. Gudgekin is saved from the horrible fate of lifelong self-absorption (which might lead her to Sartrean existentialism) by a mechanism we have seen operate elsewhere in Gardner's fiction: concern for others. Gudgekin does not swing all the way back to her original position, in which she had no concern whatever for herself; instead, she finds a middle ground from which she can participate in life as a fully functioning human being.

Intellectually, "The Griffin and the Wise Old Philosopher" is probably the most interesting of all Gardner's short stories for children, a circumstance that may well disqualify all but a handful of its intended audience from a full appreciation of the story. It would be a rarely precocious child or adolescent, I suspect, who would be prepared to deal with the Heisenberg principle, which is, on one level, the subject of the story.

The story is set in the village of "Heizenburg," at the foot of Griffin Mountain. The problem is that a griffin, by definition "an unreasonable creature," generates confusion every time he appears and observes human beings at their daily activities, with the result that whenever the griffin is around absolutely no work can be accomplished. Airplane and train schedules are hopelessly disrupted, masons can't lay bricks, carpenters can't build or electricians hook up wires, and the ferryboat pilot is stuck in the middle of the river, unable to decide which is the left bank and which the right.

The village slips toward chaos, and the king, echoing Henry II's question about Archbishop Becket, asks, "Who . . . will rid me of this damnable griffin?" (*G*, 28). He then orders a "stout, white-bearded" old philosopher, reputed to be wise, to get rid of the griffin in three days or face jail. The philosopher is comically modeled on Socrates; his wife is "an old battle-ax, or talked like one, though she loved him dearly," and he "always start[s] with the assumption that [he] know[s] nothing, and probably nobody else knows much either, however they may prattle and labor to sound convincing" (*G*, 30–31).

The problem actually solves itself, although the philosopher ultimately gets credit for the solution. The griffin is puzzled by the fact that, in spite of his close and prolonged observation of human activity, he never witnesses a single instance in which people accomplish anything. He cannot reconcile his observations with the apparent fact that humans *do* accomplish things: houses get built, bricks laid, wires connected. In utter frustration at his inability to verify human accomplishment, the griffin decides in favor of his observations and concludes that the evidence of such accomplishment is mere illusion. Coincidentally with the expiration of the philosopher's three-day term, the griffin retires in a huff to his castle, resolving never again to waste his time observing humans.

Meanwhile, the philosopher goes to the king and asks if it is not true that when people see the griffin they become so confused that they "aren't sure of *anything*." The king confirms this view and demands that the philosopher get to the point: "Have you rid me of the griffin or haven't you?" "What griffin?" the philosopher replies, and it subsequently appears that the philosopher is exactly right. There is no griffin.

This story lifts the Heisenberg principle, or "uncertainty principle," from the realm of subatomic physics and applies it more broadly to human affairs. The general statement of this principle is that the act of observing a thing alters the thing observed, so that certainty about the behavior of observed phenomena is impossible. This, of course, is what causes the griffin's problem and leads to his erroneous conclusion. He does not understand that when people are observed by a griffin they behave like people being observed by a griffin—that is, confused and incapable of doing anything—rather than like normal human beings. Ironically, it is thus the griffin's own nature that drives him away. Besides being a dramatization of the Heisenberg principle, the story also reembodies Gardner's theme of uncertainty, that we live in a world where we're "not really sure of what's going on."

The remaining two stories in *Gudgekin the Thistle Girl* are much shorter, slighter works. In "The Shape-Shifters of Shorm" the emperor is troubled by the threat of disorder posed by the otherwise harmless shape-shifters and offers as a reward for whoever can "cleanse the empire of the terrible shape-shifters . . . whatever he dare[s] to name" (*G*, 43). A knight, a wizard, and a mechanic successively undertake the quest. They all fail, in part because in the meantime a feeble old woodchopper has reasoned that, since all the people have gone to the imperial palace either to volunteer for the quest or to see how it turns out, anyone left wandering about in the empire must be one of the shape-shifters. The woodchopper therefore chops off the head of everyone he meets, including, unfortunately, the knight, wizard, and mechanic, and stuffs their heads in his sack. He then presents himself at the palace to claim his modest reward: a round-trip ticket to Brussels for a short vacation (the knight, wizard, and mechanic had asked, respectively, for half the empire, half the empire and the emperor's daughter's hand in marriage, and the whole empire and the daughter's hand).

The woodchopper has, it is true, the heads of all the shape-shifters, but when the emperor also finds the heads of the knight, wizard, and mechanic, he accuses the woodchopper of murder and sentences him to hang. When the woodchopper asks if this means he doesn't get his vacation, the emperor reconsiders and grants a reprieve: the woodchopper may go to Brussels, in handcuffs, but he must swear not to escape and agree to be hanged when he returns. The woodchopper agrees, but after he has been in Brussels a mere three days, "he suddenly bolted down an alley and escaped, and he changed his name to Zobrowski and dropped out of sight" (*G*, 52).

Cowart finds this "needlessly sanguinary" story less satisfying than others and interprets it as "an ecological fable, for the killing of the Shape-Shifters involves also the killing of three innocents" (Cowart, 136). This view seems a bit off the mark, at least in regard to the "three innocents" (whose motives convict them of avarice, a mortal sin), since knights, wizards, and mechanics are a dime a dozen, whereas the shape-shifters surely represent a unique life-form and appear to be entirely innocuous. Although Cowart finds both this story and the next one relatively deficient in humor and "astute psychological observation," it seems to me that "The Shape-Shifters" has plenty of both The humor is subtler, perhaps, than in other stories, and is somewhat darkly tinged, but it is assuredly present. The story's message, presumably, again concerns uncertainty and its potentially dire consequences, as represented in the difficulty of distinguishing shape-shifters from normal people. As far as psychological insight is concerned, the story has much to offer on the mental processes and behavior of emperors, "average" people (the mob who flock to the palace), and condemned men released on their own recognizance.

The last story, "The Sea Gulls," is less than four pages long, despite the fact that its plot spans fourteen years. A king, caught by an ogre, shoots dice for his life with the stipulation that if the king wins (which he does, by cheating), he will enjoy a respite of seven years, after which the ogre may eat both him and his children. When that term is up, the king makes a similar deal with a witch, who, after seven more years, will feed the king and his three sons and one daughter to her geese. The witch turns into a giant owl and eats the ogre "like a dumpling" when he appears. Seven years later, the king can find no one to help him, and his children flee to the woods, where they meet a hermit who advises them that the way to escape the witch is to turn themselves into sea gulls by reciting a magic verse. The only catch is that they will be gulls forever; not "all the magic in Lapland" can turn them back into children. The witch arrives and the three sons immediately (and foolishly) say the verse and are transformed. The daughter, realizing that "forever is too long," stands her ground: "I would rather be eaten by a goose than turn into a sea gull forever."

She thereby pulls a magic trigger, and the hermit turns into a prince, who marries the girl and later helps her throw old bread crumbs to her hapless brothers, who spend the rest of forever flying around and irritably crying, "Lost! Lost!" The king, ominously, is never seen again. The mechanism by which these developments work is that the witch had once turned the prince into a hermit until he could encounter "someone with a proper sense of values—for instance, someone who knew that, whatever one might think at first glance, people are better than sea gulls" (*G*, 59). Cowart correctly identifies the story's message as the lesson that "one ought not to mortgage the future for the present, especially if one must lie and cheat into the bargain" (Cowart, 136).

The King of the Hummingbirds and Other Tales

In "The King of the Hummingbirds," Olaf, youngest son of a coppersmith, possesses the virtue of always being able to see a situation from the other person's side, a quality that gains him many friends among both animals and human beings. When he encounters the dying King of the Hummingbirds, that monarch, impressed by Olaf's kindly face, makes him his heir, passing to him the ring that will identify him to the flock as ruler. Olaf keeps silent about his royal status, but it will stand him in good stead later.

The king habitually walks about with his daughter in a walled garden, until one day the thorn of a rose gets caught in the lock on the garden gate, trapping the princess inside. The thorn dries and stiffens, blowing sand seals the crack, and honeybees are attracted to the wall, in turn attracting bears. Half the kingdom and the princess's hand to whoever can open the gate. Among other losers, Olaf's two brothers accept the challenge, the first packing dynamite around the gate. He is chased away by a bear before he can push the plunger. When the first brother's "intelligent" solution fails, the second attempts the problem with "style." He decorates the gate with orchids and charges at it with a golden battering ram. The orchids attract a couple of bears, who chase him away.

Olaf's turn comes, and he stalls, trying to figure out what to do. Being stupid, he hasn't a clue. He rolls up his sleeves, then removes his shirt, inadvertently revealing the royal ring on a string around his neck. Soon, thousands of hummingbirds surround him. Their droning draws the bees from their hives, creating a commotion, and the wind from their wings blows the sand out of the crack, allowing honey to drip down on the lock. Moistened by honey, the thorn bends and the lock springs open. The bears rush out of the garden, spooking the second brother's majestic white horse so that it falls on the first brother's dynamite plunger and blows bears, orchids, and bees sky-high. The princess, rescued, emerges and exclaims, "Wow!" (*H*, 15). Somewhat anticlimactically, Olaf and the princess will be married.

Cowart's reading of this story as a psychosexual allegory can hardly be improved upon. Identifying the underlying theme as "growing up and dealing with the opposite sex," Cowart explores the story's connections with the medieval *Romance of the Rose,* in which "the hero desires a symbolic rose located at the heart of a garden patrolled by allegorical personages . . . who represent emotional or social aids and hindrances to the consummation of his love" and, "at the poem's climax . . . reaches the rose and pokes his staff into the little grotto that shelters it." In Gardner's story the "lock must be lubricated with a viscous fluid" that softens "that clitoral thorn" before the garden can be penetrated, as the "suggestive collection of birds and bees" hovers over the scene. Cowart also notes that the "penetration" is "followed by the action of a plunger and an orgasmic explosion." The lesson is that the "young readers" can also someday "open some refractory gate, sexual or otherwise, if they have first cultivated certain pleasing habits of personality" (Cowart, 136–37).

Most readers would agree with Cowart that the next story, "The Witch's Wish" is one of Gardner's funniest. The scene in which the witch and a former prince transformed to a toad must, as Cowart puts it, "watch their language around a trigger-happy and not very bright wishing pool surrounded by the tombstones of those who thoughtlessly complained, 'I wish I were dead,'" is genuinely hilarious at the same time that it conveys one of the story's principal lessons: that if one finds oneself in an uncongenial career or way of life, other options are available.

The story concerns a witch accidentally converted during a visit to a church or synagogue (she doesn't notice which) she intends to burn down later. Convicted of her sins, she resolves to stop being a witch and instead to sell paper flowers on the street and give all her money to the poor. She visits the queen of the witches to inquire about resigning but is unable to identify the denomination or even the religion to which she has been converted—a matter of great importance to the queen, who remains a horrible witch in spite of having been converted sixty-seven times. Gardner's message here is an ecumenical one, suggesting that the importance of religion lies not in doctrinal or sectarian matters but in the power (and pleasure) of doing good.

The queen is sympathetic but can offer no direct way out, informing her subject that "you can't stop being a witch just because you want to. It's against the rules, like trying to stop being a Mormon" (*H*, 24). She does, however, suggest with a wink that the witch "take the shortcut home." The shortcut lies through the forest and brings the witch to the wishing pool and her interview with the prince-turned-toad. The toad had wished his transformation, having been unhappy and incompetent as a prince, but he is also unhappy as a toad. Upon learning the joys—as he sees them—of a witch's life, he wishes he were a witch and becomes the happiest witch in the kingdom, as the witch wishes she were a sweet old lady selling flowers and giving her money to the poor and instantly becomes one. Although it is a hard life, she is "serenely happy, for doing good nearly always makes people happy" (*H*, 30).

"The Pear Tree" is also rollicking good fun, though the moral is harder to spot. The king has decreed, for obscure reasons, that his daughter will marry whoever presents her with a single perfect pear. The king and queen of the elves, who are all Jewish, turn the kingdom's only perfect pear tree into a dewdrop and conceal it in a rose, which frustrates the designs of a series of suitors, including a knight, a merchant, and a poet, who all reject the rose for one reason or another. The poet delivers himself of a delightful parody of William Blake's

"The Sick Rose" and considers taking the rose to the princess "as a metaphor of the shortness of life and the certainty of failure" but concludes that the princess would "never get it" and goes on his way (*H*, 35).

The unlikely hero is Eddie (mistakenly identified by Cowart as "Irving," who is a Jewish elf mentioned at the end of the story), the fat, bookish, bespectacled only son of a poor Jewish blacksmith. On the advice of his mother, Eddie takes up the suit. Although he is disappointed that the pear tree seems to be gone, Eddie takes the rose rejected by the others and eventually gives it to the princess, first having to get it past the black palace guards, who speak in jive. The dewdrop then turns back into the pear tree, and Eddie's suit is successful.

Cowart reads the story as "a fantasy about the instrumentality responsible for happy betrothals" and classes it thematically with "The King of the Hummingbirds" as a story about dealing with the opposite sex (Cowart, 137–38). The story also has something to say about relations among different ethnic and religious groups and the benefits that may accrue from acting on motives other than self-interest.

The last story in the collection, "The Gnome and the Dragon," is by long odds the most difficult, leading Cowart to conclude that it "will probably baffle or frustrate any child who reads or hears it, for it really speaks directly to the adult who has read a good deal of Gardner's adult fiction." Certainly no child and few adults are likely to make complete sense of this story, but then I am not sure that children require the world of entertaining fiction to make complete sense; that seems rather to be a distinctly adult demand, as it is about the world at large. Nevertheless, as Cowart points out, the story is at some level a familiar Gardnerian "parable about art's responsibility to deal with those dragons of terrible reality" (Cowart, 139).

The gnome is a "great artist" in whose hands reality is like putty, "as it would be in the hands of a whittler or a fiddler or a teller of moralizing tales" (*H*, 47). By the magic of his art the gnome can change himself or anything else—except dragons, which terrify him—into whatever he pleases. The gnome (whose abilities and actions are to be identified with those of the author, who has wrought his gnome magic in all the preceding stories) has made so many transformations of reality that even he is no longer sure about what is what. Meanwhile, dragons are overrunning the kingdom, so that the king makes the standard offer to whoever can get rid of them. Through an ingenious series of twists, the gnome and his only friend, a billy goat who covets the princess's hand, so terrify the dragons by their appearance that the dragons run into one another and explode. Afterward, the king denies the existence of dragons and says he never made any offer. The billy goat is frustrated and angry, suddenly realizing that the king is none other than the gnome and that he has been tricked. Then he remembers that, as a result of a prior transformation, the gnome is also himself, and so is the princess.

The nature of reality, the story seems to say, is a tricky business in which it is impossible to be absolutely certain of anything, thus restating the general theme of all the stories. All the characters and events, in this story and the others, are the products of the artist's magic. As for the dragons, they may well represent recalcitrant and unpleasant realities—"the blunt facts of our mortality," as Gardner elsewhere calls them—but our most effective weapon against them is the transforming power of art.

The Art of Living and Other Stories

Gardner's second and last collection of adult short fiction, *The Art of Living and Other Stories* (1981), presents ten stories, eight of which had been previously published in a variety of magazines and journals over the preceding seven years. The longest story, "Vlemk the Box-Painter," had been published as a separate book in 1979. Thus only the title story, strategically placed at the end of the collection, appears in print for the first time.

As was usual with Gardner's works, the initial critical response from reviewers ranged from scathing, even contemptuous condemnation to the highest praise, both for the collection as a whole and for individual stories. Still, the reviews were preponderantly favorable. Of some sixty-one substantive reviews summarized in Robert Morace's *John Gardner: An Annotated Secondary Bibliography*, thirty-eight may be described as favorable, sixteen as mixed, and only seven as unfavorable, representing approximate percentages for the three categories as follows: favorable, 62.3 percent; mixed, 26.2 percent; unfavorable, 11.5 percent (Morace, 186–98). Interestingly, this distribution almost duplicates reviewers' response to *The King's Indian:* favorable, 62.6 percent; mixed, 20.8 percent; unfavorable, 16.6 percent (Morace, 104–12). Critics David Cowart and Gregory Morris, each of whom devotes a chapter to *The Art of Living*, obviously regard the stories as successful examples of the author's fiction, finding them both artistically and thematically of a piece with the longer works.

As remarked earlier, the ten stories in *The Art of Living* possess a striking thematic coherence, considering their independent composition. The unifying theme, which variously embodies most of Gardner's other characteristic themes, is implied by the title. It is the relationship between life and art—a relationship that, both in Gardner's aesthetic theory and in his broader view of human affairs, is of paramount importance. Both Cowart and Morris recognize and explore this relationship, "the collection's master theme," as Cowart calls it (Cowart, 165). Cowart finds, additionally, an underlying musical principle of organization among the stories; his chapter on *The Art of Living* is entitled

"Theme and Variations," and he discusses in detail the prominence of music and musical organization in individual stories ("Nimram," "Redemption," "The Music Lover," "Come on Back") and in the collection as a whole.

Gardner's belief that life imitates art more profoundly than art imitates life is the keystone of his theory of moral art. The artist—the Shaper, as Gardner calls him in the novel *Grendel*, translating the Old English word for "poet," *scop*—is he who provides the visions his culture will value and emulate. Accordingly, if the artist's productions are "good," then society, culture, and civilization will become good; if they are "bad," society will become debased and degenerate. In Gardner's terms, "good art" implies not merely technical virtuosity but a moral dimension as well. Good art must ultimately be affirmative and life enhancing, while bad art cheapens and negates life. At its worst, it fosters nihilism and despair. Gardner's moral aesthetic is perhaps summed up most succinctly in the definition of a good book he offers in his controversial tract *On Moral Fiction*: "A good book is one that, for its time, is wise, sane, and magical, one that clarifies life and tends to improve it" (*OMF*, 132).

Gardner's large claims for the influence art has on life are debatable, of course, but within the terms of his aesthetic system that influence is a given condition. An interesting corollary is that, at least in Gardner's fiction, characters do "make life art." A part of Gardner's message is often identified by critics as the proposition that we should make life art. This interpretation seems not precisely accurate. Rather, Gardner assumes that people shape their lives by principles that are essentially aesthetic, and the important questions then involve choice of principles, specific strategies for enacting them, and the quality (good or bad) of the "art" produced. These are the matters dramatized in Gardner's fiction generally; they are treated most specifically in the stories in this collection.

"Nimram"

Like all of Gardner's fiction, the final published version of "Nimram" was the product of extensive revision, as materials in the Gardner Papers collection at the University of Rochester clearly show (boxes B-8 and B-14). Besides minor textual revisions, these materials reveal that the title character was originally to be named Benjamin Amram. Moreover, a note at the foot of a manuscript page explains that "The charac[ter] Benjamin Amram is to some extent modeled on, and . . . a tribute to Maestro Zubin Mehta; nevertheless, the story, and nearly everything about Amram and his wife, is pure fiction" (box B-14). The same manuscript also reveals a succession of rejected titles for the story. "Wings and Prayers" appears first as a title but is crossed out; then "The Dream of Transcendence" appears, also crossed out; finally "Amram" appears as the title, awaiting only the author's change of the character's name to "Nimram."

Benjamin Nimram is a supremely successful symphony orchestra conductor at the peak of his career. His life, "a joy to him," has been an unbroken string of "one resounding success after another," and he is universally regarded as "a genius." In his private thoughts, he accepts his success with philosophical fatalism: he is "a fortunate accident, a man supremely lucky"; he has "been dealt all high cards" and regards himself as "one of the elect" (*AL*, 7–8).

Nimram's serene acceptance of his good fortune is challenged when he meets a terminally ill teenage girl on an evening flight from Los Angeles to Chicago. Occupying adjacent seats, the two converse, Nimram seeking to allay the girl's fear of flying. It turns out that the girl is a musician too, playing in her school orchestra. Her life, however, contrasts with Nimram's. She has been dealt low cards, and although she is of course not happy with her "terminal" condition, she accepts it with a stoic fatalism very much like Nimram's acceptance of his good luck. "If you're chosen, you're chosen," she says, ironically counterpointing Nimram's sense of being one of the "elect" (*AL*, 14).

Nimram keenly senses the disparity between his life and the girl's, his sympathy complicated by the fact that the girl bears a strong resemblance to Nimram's wife. He feels sorrow, of course, for the girl and her parents, and apparently some measure of unconscious guilt for his good fortune, but he principally feels "only a profound embarrassment and helplessness"; he is "helplessly fortunate and therefore unfit, unworthy, his whole life light and unprofitable as a puff-ball, needless as ascending smoke" (*AL*, 19).

The following night, the girl, Anne Curtis, and her parents attend when Nimram conducts the Chicago Symphony in Mahler's Fifth. The concert symbolically re-creates the flight from Los Angeles, embodying a message—the story's theme—of redemption or salvation through art. The orchestra fills the stage "like some monstrous black creature too enormous to fly," awaiting the conductor, who comes "like a panther," "bound[s] to the podium," turns, bows, opens the score and studies it "like a man reading dials and gauges of infinite complexity." He is the "pilot" who will stir the "creature" to flight. As the music begins, it seems to Ann Curtis "a vast sweep . . . as smooth and sharp-edged as an enormous scythe—she had never in her life heard a sound so broad, as if all of humanity, living and dead, had come together for one grand onslaught. The sound ran, gathering its strength, along the ground, building in intensity, full of doubt, even terror, but also fury, and then—amazingly, quite easily—lifted" (*AL*, 26–29).

The plane, flying through storm and darkness, was a sort of airborne Noah's ark, carrying its passengers to salvation. This is suggested when the girl, conversing with Nimram, quotes her Uncle Charley as having said that "the most interesting thing about Noah's Ark is that all the animals on it were scared and stupid" (*AL*, 23). The orchestra and concert hall become a musical analogue to the airplane and the ark, carrying the musicians and the audience to a serenity beyond death (suggested by the image of the "enormous scythe").

The story's climax is the moment the music "lifts off." This is the artistic moment, the moment when life and art interpenetrate and the prospect of redemption by art shines through. It is a moment that recurs, in various forms, in most of the stories in *The Art of Living*. The participants in the artistic moment are "all of humanity, living and dead," a convocation that recalls similar gatherings in the novels *Nickel Mountain* and *Mickelsson's Ghosts* and that will be repeated in the artistic moment of the final story in the collection.

"Redemption"

"Redemption" (titled "Escape" in an early draft) is one of the most intensely autobiographical of all Gardner's fictions. Although he changed the names of the characters and altered details of the action to suit his fictional purposes, the story is essentially Gardner's account of the childhood accident in which his younger brother Gilbert died. As Howell has demonstrated in "The Wound and the Albatross: John Gardner's Apprenticeship," this tragic event, and Gardner's sense of responsibility and guilt for it, had a profound influence on Gardner's fiction throughout his career.[33]

The inciting event in "Redemption"—the accident—generally follows the outline of the real event in Gardner's life. Jack Hawthorne, age twelve, is driving a tractor pulling a two-ton, sod-crushing roller called a cultipacker. His brother, David, age seven, is riding on the cultipacker, and his five-year-old sister, Phoebe, is riding on the fender of the tractor. David falls off and is crushed by the roller, as Jack watches in horror, unable to think clearly enough to try to stop the machine. Jack's sense of guilt is caused by his belief that "even at the last moment he could have prevented his brother's death by slamming on the tractor's brakes . . . but he was unable to think, or, rather, thought unclearly, and so watched it happen, as he would again and again watch it happen in his mind, with nearly undiminished intensity and clarity, all his life," and by the fact that he was not supposed to permit the younger children to ride on the machines (*AL*, 30).

The effects of the tragedy on the family are dire. The father, Dale Hawthorne, is so wracked by grief that he abandons the farm periodically, riding off for days or weeks at a time on his motorcycle, pursuing meaningless love affairs and contemplating suicide. The mother, though "so sapped by grief that she could barely move her arms," somehow finds the strength to "move step by step past disaster and in the end keep her family from wreck," comforting her surviving children as she can and "forcing" on them "comforts more permanent: piano and, for Jack, French-horn lessons, school and church activities, above all an endless, exhausting ritual of chores" (*AL*, 32–33).

The story is narrated from Jack's perspective and principally concerns his coming to terms with his sorrow and guilt. He rejects the comfort offered by the community of family and friends and throws himself into his farm work, alternately raging and grieving alone in the fields. As he has done before, he makes up stories as he drives the tractor, but now his stories have changed: no longer are his themes those of sexual conquest and heroic battle; now his "fantasies came to be all of self-sacrifice, pitiful stories in which he redeemed his life by throwing it away to save others more worthwhile." Eventually he recognizes the falseness of these fantasies—"the manipulation of shame to buy love"—and they no longer help; his sense of worthlessness increases until he begins to think of suicide. Even communion with the natural world, in which he has taken some comfort, finally proves inadequate to assuage his grief.

When Jack's father, in control of his grief at last, returns to the family fold after a protracted absence, Jack feels only rage and hatred. He turns to the French horn "more and more to escape their herding warmth," playing third chair in the Batavia Civic Orchestra and riding a bus to Rochester on Saturdays "to take lessons from Arcady Yegudkin, 'the General,' at the Eastman School of Music." Yegudkin is a

Russian refugee who had played horn in the orchestra of the czar before the revolution. As Howell points out, Yegudkin, although a great musician, is himself isolated from humanity by his pride and absorption in the "single truth" of his music; he is "the personification of the self-absorbed and self-reflexive artist that Jack is in danger of becoming and that Gardner was at this time criticizing in the early chapters of *On Moral Fiction*" (Howell, 1985, 6).

Thus when the "artistic moment" comes—when Yegudkin tries out a new horn at the end of Jack's lesson—Jack's redemption is effected through what Howell calls an "ironic variation on the traditional epiphany." When Yegudkin's stunning performance breaks off suddenly, the room continues to shimmer. Jack asks, without thinking, "You think I'll ever play like that?" Yegudkin laughs at the absurdity of the thought, and Jack is shocked back to a more mundane reality. He leaves the studio weeping and joins the "dazed-looking Saturday-morning shoppers herding along irritably, meekly, through painfully bright light" (*AL*, 47–48). He will return home to the "herding warmth" of family and friends, the community of comfort his pride and self-absorption had previously rejected. He will not play like Yegudkin, but the reader may sense, remembering the stories Jack makes up and tells himself on the tractor, that there are other artistic avenues open to him.

"Stillness"

Like "Redemption," "Stillness" is a story Gardner mined from the pages of an unfinished autobiographical novel (posthumously published as *Stillness*); in "Stillness," however, he retained the original fictional names for himself and his wife: Martin and Joan Orrick. His revisions consisted of some rearrangement of passages and the addition of the last four paragraphs of the story.

The story is narrated entirely from Joan's point of view, which in view of the story's autobiographical nature and the fact that the author appears as the other major character, sets up an interesting aesthetic distance between the author and his work. The story's outer frame, or "envelope," concerns Joan and Martin's driving through St. Louis and stopping for the night at a motel on the other side of the city. They are traveling to Oklahoma, where he will serve as a judge for a book award. Their drive through the inner city—where in their college days, before their marriage, Joan had worked as a piano player at the Duggers

School of the Dance—releases a powerful flood of memories for Joan and, in combination with the drugs she must take for the pain associated with a chronic illness, triggers a bizarre mental experience that unites times and persons decades apart.

As they drive through blighted, almost deserted downtown St. Louis, Joan muses on what it would be like to have "second sight" and to have foreseen, twenty-five years ago, the ruin and desolation that would descend on the once-thriving, bustling heart of the city. With the clarity of a vision, she imagines herself as the late-1940s schoolgirl she once was, suddenly swept forward in time to the St. Louis of the mid-1970s. Her consciousness divides, part remaining in the car in present time and part seeing through the eyes of her younger self on the street. That younger self, "the imaginary Joan," she imagines would think, "I'm in the future! . . . and there's been some terrible war, or a plague, and everything's been ruined" (*AL*, 51). Joan wishes she could communicate with her younger self, reassure her somehow, and indeed this almost happens. The girl recognizes her older self, and for a moment Joan is able to see herself from the perspective of her own past. The moment passes, however, as present reality reasserts itself. Second sight and other psychic phenomena, as well as the interpenetration of distantly separate times, are frequent concerns in Gardner's longer fiction, though they are not so prevalent in the short stories.

Joan's vision of the past looking at the future leads into the story's inner part, as they drive past the now-fire-gutted building that housed the dance studio where Joan once worked and where Martin had occasionally visited her, riding in on his motorcycle from college in Indiana. She reminisces in detail about the ballet teacher she worked for, Jacqui Duggers, and her husband, Pete, who taught tap dancing. Joan's strongest memory, and the aesthetic center of the story, is of a particular technique Pete Duggers would use in his tap dancing. He would start slowly, his feet moving "as if swinging by themselves, as if his body were suspended like a puppet's," his taps "light and quick, as if he never put his weight down with either foot," and then build, "with elegant shuffles and turns, then more speed, and more, and more and still more until it seemed that the room spun drunkenly, crazily" (*AL*, 54).

The climax of Pete's dance, "what was truly miraculous, so that it made you catch your breath, was the way he could stop, completely relaxed, leaning his elbow on empty air and grinning as if he'd been standing there for hours, all that movement and sound you'd been hearing pure phantom and illusion." It is a "sudden stillness like an escape from reality," a suspension of ordinary reality through which the realm of pure art shines. In that moment, he "stood perfectly still, the piano was still, his young students gaped, and then abruptly reality came back as the piano tinkled lightly and he listlessly danced and, as he did so, leaned toward his students and winked. 'You see? Stillness! That's the magic!'" (*AL*, 54–55).

This is the artistic moment, a moment of transcendent serenity in which mundane dwellers may catch a glimpse of the ideal. It is analogous to the shimmering moment in "Redemption" when Yegudkin suddenly breaks off his virtuoso performance on the French horn in the middle of a note, and to the moment in "Nimram" when the music, the orchestra, and the concert hall suddenly lift off the ground, as well as to similar moments in most of the other stories in *The Art of Living*.

In the four paragraphs Gardner added to this story when he lifted it from his unfinished novel, the outer frame reasserts itself. Joan and Martin have stopped at a motel west of the city for the night. Martin has gone to bed. Joan's thoughts return to the relationship between past and future. She thinks of her grandmother, who reputedly had second sight, now gone, as the Homer of a paper her husband has recently delivered is gone. And as for the future, she realizes as she drifts toward sleep that "sooner or later everyone, of course, knows the future" (*AL*, 64).

"The Music Lover"

One of the shortest stories in the collection, "The Music Lover" is actually a parable or fable thinly disguised as a realistic story. Told by an unidentified third-person narrator and set "some years ago" in the otherwise unidentified "our city," the story centers on the elderly, retired Professor Alfred Klingman, the "music lover" of the title. Klingman's late wife was a piano teacher, and the single, consuming pleasure of his life is attending concerts as he used to do with his wife. Although "singularly uninformed" about the technical aspects of music and unable to "identify by number and key any symphony but Beethoven's Fifth, and even in that case he could never recall the key," Professor Klingman enjoys the music he hears as much as anyone possibly could. He even seems to have an intuitive grasp of musical "jokes." Indeed, his obtrusive emotional responses to the music irritate other concertgoers and make him an object of some mockery and ridicule to rude children and the malicious.

The critical event of the story comes when Klingman attends a concert advertised as presenting "three contemporary pieces." The first is a cello concerto in which the soloist uses a saw instead of a bow and saws the cello in two. The second features two radios blaring at each other on different stations as a violinist expresses his "musical impressions of a life-sized photograph of an ape" (*AL*, 68–69). Mercifully, Klingman (and the reader) is saved from the third "contemporary piece" by intermission, and he flees in vocal horror to the lobby. In an extreme example of the influence of art (bad art, in this case) on life, Klingman almost suffers heart failure as a result of his outrageous experience.

A stranger follows Klingman to the lobby, leads him to the lounge, buys him a drink, and sits to talk with him. The stranger is "a thin, sallow person of thirty-five or forty, dressed in a black suit with a black waistcoat and black bow tie. His forehead was high and queerly narrow, like the forehead of a horse, and his eyes, which blinked continually, were unnaturally bright and alert, like a chicken's" (*AL*, 73). He turns out to be the composer, of course, and his attributes of dress and physical appearance link him iconographically with Gardner's other anarchists and nihilists.

The man has sensed that perhaps Klingman "alone, in all that fat, complacent audience, understood tonight's music" and attempts to explain why he composes as he does. It is significant that he despises his audience, in Gardner's fiction an unfailing mark of the bad artist. The composer recounts at length his lifetime of repeated disappointment and disillusionment. The actual experience of life has never measured up to the ideals of joy and sorrow—"divine virtue or hair-raising wickedness," "ravishing loveliness or consummate horror," "intoxicating bliss" or "undreamt-of anguish" (*AL*, 74)—implied by books and by "large words for good and evil." He is in exactly the position of the anarchist Josef Mallin in "The Warden": unable to affirm either the desire for aesthetic wholeness or the limitations of ordinary reality. Convinced that ideals are false and illusory and hating the logical restraints of time, place, and physicality, he makes Mallin's "natural mistake" and "goes at the universe with dynamite sticks" (*KI*, 114). Thus Gardner "translates" the art of living in a political state (in "The Warden") into the art of music in this story. The message, however, remains the same.

As the young man's story sinks in, and the young man seems to grow angrier by the minute, a subtle change comes over Professor Klingman, who has, after all, "spent a lifetime teaching the young and outraged." Beginning with the observation that his wife had been a piano teacher, Klingman begins, "slowly and patiently, to explain what she had meant to him, though of course his feeling was impossible to put into words" (*AL*, 76). Klingman's explanation implicitly denies the composer's belief that such feelings do not exist, and the fact that the feelings are essentially inexpressible effectively belies the composer's contention that "human need for communication has found itself a way to create sounds that lie beyond" the limitation imposed by the "poverty of actual life" (*AL*, 75). Klingman's own life proves that a man's reach does exceed his grasp, and the composer's inability to understand this point is the measure of his emotional maiming and the badness of his art.

"Trumpeter"

Thematically, "Trumpeter" is the concluding installment of the "Queen Louisa" stories begun in *The King's Indian*. The story traces the evolution of the queen's sweeping social and political reforms to its logical culmination in "a balanced kingdom, the only kingdom in the world where art reigned supreme" (*AL*, 87). Thus "Trumpeter" offers a fabulistic example of Gardner's claims regarding the benefits of living according to aesthetic principles, or "making life art."

This story is fablelike in all senses of the word commonly recognized by dictionaries (except the sense in which *fable* means "a lie or falsehood"): it is concise, it makes a cautionary or exemplary point, and it features an animal in a prominent role. This last feature is perhaps the most remarkable thing about the story from a technical perspective. The entire story is narrated from the point of view of the palace dog, Trumpeter, a circumstance that places the story in a modern tradition of fictional attempts to render animal consciousness. That tradition includes such entries as Ernest Hemingway's rendition of the lion's consciousness in "The Short, Happy Life of Francis Macomber," Ted Mooney's striking representation of dolphin consciousness in the novel *Easy Travel to Other Planets*, and Charles Johnson's narration from a German shepherd's point of view in his story "Menagerie, a Child's Fable."[34]

Although the reader is reminded one way or another in every paragraph that the events of the story are flowing through the dog's mind and represent his perceptions and memories, this knowledge does not overwhelm the events themselves. Indeed, Gardner walks a fine line in the balance between technique and content in this story, with the result that the two constantly comment on each other, generating ironies and tensions that account for much of the story's dynamic effect. Generally, the dog's literal-mindedness (his inability to recognize or understand "art") and intellectual limitations leave the reader to infer the nature and significance of events beyond the dog's comprehension. For example, when Queen Louisa supposedly transforms herself periodically into a toad, Trumpeter sees no change whatever in the queen and must himself infer what has "happened" from changes in the behavior of others toward the queen. He is also unable to imagine events at which he was not actually present, so that, although he remembers the original princess's gradual decline into pallor and weakness, he has no clear idea of what became of her, having been forcibly banished from her sickroom before her death.

Trumpeter is aware of most of his limitations, linguistic and otherwise. He acknowledges that "man's ways are not dog's" and is "befuddled" by sentences, although he has no difficulty understanding single words. He is also aware of his limited canine perspective in regard to time. Thus he cannot be certain whether the peasant boys and girls Louisa has adopted as princes and princesses are really her children, since, as he thinks, "the life of a dog is but a heartbeat, so to speak, in the long span of man." (Gardner thus renders, incidentally, the insight of Robert Frost's poem "The Span of Life" from the perspective of the dog.) Trumpeter does, however, understand (intuitively rather than rationally) that by making the peasants her children, "the Queen had brought happiness to a kingdom that had suffered, before that, grave troubles—peasants against royalty, 'madness against madness,' as the minstrel said: an obscure saying; but Trumpeter, in his heart, understood it" (*AL*, 80).

The dog's chief limitation, which highlights a major point of the story, is his total inability to recognize the difference between art and life. He has watched in bafflement while the entire court would "sit erect for hours, dead silent except for an occasional whisper, an occasional cough, listening to people on a bright raised platform howl." When he companionably tried to join the howlers, he remembers, he was kicked and sent outside, and when he had seen, on the same platform "a man in black creep up cunningly on another, a dagger in his hand, and when he, Trumpeter, had hurtled to the rescue, he'd been beaten and seized by five knights and had been chained behind the buttery" (*AL*, 79).

Queen Louisa realizes her mad dream of turning the entire kingdom into a work of art. She eliminates—or denatures—crime by inviting the cutpurses and pirates to guard the royal treasury, and she levels social inequity and ends exploitation by marrying off her newfound princesses to merchants and their servants and her princes to merchants' daughters. Even Vrokror the Terrible, embodiment of anarchy and nihilism and therefore the greatest threat of all, is redeemed by marriage to the "new" Princess Muriel.

Peace and justice thus prevail in Gregor's kingdom, "the only kingdom in the world where art reigned supreme." This idea is suggested symbolically, along with the implication that things may not be so well elsewhere, by a characteristically Gardnerian image of light contrasting with darkness: "The palace was full of light—beyond the windows, thick darkness." The benefits of artistic life are accessible only to human beings, apparently, since Trumpeter, uncomprehending, flees "away from the dancing and light, away from the joyful celebration of things that he knew to be quite proper, and when he reached the depths of the forest, he began to howl" (*AL*, 87). While Trumpeter's howl is unmistakably animal in nature, it is also the howl of anguished humanity denied the consoling, illuminating power of art.

"The Library Horror"

"The Library Horror" is one of Gardner's most difficult fictions. Narrated by a man who doubts his sanity (he is descended from a long line of lunatics, he says, and his father is in an asylum) and who thinks he is dying from wounds inflicted on him by a fictional character, the story seems to concern the relationship between "ordinary" reality and the kind of reality represented in works of fiction.

The narrator, Winfred, is a wealthy recluse who has systematically isolated himself from virtually all human contact. He makes only "rare official visits" to his bank and otherwise seldom leaves his home and library. He does not own an automobile, since to do so "would inevitably involve me with a mechanic for the engine, a chauffeur, and heaven knows what else" (*AL*, 89). He finds excuses for failing to visit his father at the asylum (a source of guilt), and he has only minimal contact with his wife, Greer. According to Cowart's analysis, Winfred commits the fallacy of believing that fiction is superior to real life; he retreats into a fantasy world "remote from the responsibilities of real life" and "neglects the 'art of living'" (Cowart, 176). Appropriately, he is "punished" by an agent of justice from the realm of fiction.

The crisis in Winfred's madness is triggered, ironically, by a book on aesthetics, evidently Suzanne Langer's *Problems of Art*.[35] As Winfred summarizes the book's argument, "in paintings, as in mirrors, we see 'virtual space,' that is, space that seems as real as any other until the moment we try to enter it"; similarly, in "reading novels, we move through virtual landscapes, watching virtual human beings, people who speak and act as do real human beings until they vanish, or, rather, snap magically into words on a page." The "apparitions" of music or fiction are therefore "not at all mere imitations, like the figures in a mirror"; instead, "they are created expressions of life itself," functioning "in the same ways as do other living things . . . pushed and pulled by the same laws that push and pull me or, for instance, my wife, Greer. I speak only, of course, of such works as we call successful, works that have 'vitality' or 'autonomous life'" (*AL*, 90).

Coupled with the doubt cast on our commonsensical notions of physical reality by modern theoretical physics, the ideas in the book on aesthetics strike Winfred as literal fact. He has the book in his hand when he is drawn into his tomblike library by a "particularly loud crash." He has been hearing strange noises from the library for several days, and although he normally avoids the library, he is at last compelled by some force he does not understand to go in and investigate.

What he finds in the library is that the boundaries between the world of fiction and the world of reality have vanished and the two worlds now interpenetrate. Literary characters, apparently in the flesh but only about four feet tall, begin emerging from the stacks: Raskolnikov, who menaces Winfred with his ax before being led off by "an 'outlaw' English schoolgirl," who may be Thackeray's Becky Sharp; Captain Ahab, arguing tediously with "Boswell's Dr. Johnson"; Scrooge and "Bunyan's Pilgrim," who "sound remarkably alike" to Winfred; and he talks with Jane Austen's Emma, who is not so pretty as he had imagined and seems "oddly bigoted" (*AL*, 93–94).

Engrossed in these matters, Winfred ignores his seductive wife's summons to bed, as well as her reminder that "tomorrow is visitor's day at the asylum" and he should plan to visit his father. Upon that reminder, a ball of light, "as if summoned by her words," comes shrieking at him from the books. It is Achilles, the "hero of absolute justice, God-sent doom, terrible purgation" of his youthful reading, and he has a sword. In spite of Winfred's protest that he is "not guilty!" the avenging Achilles strikes twice at his neck, inflicting mortal wounds.

Convinced that he is dying, but also entertaining the possibility that he is "going mad," Winfred speculates on the relations between fiction and reality. It seems "certainly true" to him that "if a fictional character, namely Achilles, can make blood run down my chest . . . then a living character . . . can be made to live forever, simply by being put in a fiction." Acknowledging that possibly he is "making some outlandish mistake," he nevertheless constructs a fictional dialogue between his wife and his father, as if to immortalize them by way of making amends for his neglect. But the scene he has constructed suggests an adulterous affair between the wife and father, and Winfred notes with alarm that Achilles, now "dressed in a drab suit, like a Jehovah's witness," seems to have "grasped the situation between my wife and my father." The implication is that Achilles may punish the wife and father as he has punished Winfred, and Winfred pleads, "No justice . . . enough of justice!" (*AL,* 96–100).

In Gardner's fiction, when a character senses that he is "making some outlandish mistake" or has a thought or insight that won't quite come clear, it is nearly always a significant clue to the story's meaning, as it was in the cases of Pick's nagging uneasiness about the anarchist bomber in his church in "Pastoral Care," Gregor's sense of "fundamental error" in "King Gregor and the Fool," and Gustav's insight about democracy that changes the course of history in *Freddy's Book.* Similarly, Winfred's sense of error is an indication that he is, of course, quite mad, and more importantly, that he has horribly abused the relationship between art and life. By retreating completely into the world of fiction, he has substituted art for life rather than living in approximation to art. He has thus denied and negated life, which makes him no better than a nihilist. His guilt, like that of the title character in "The Warden," is mortal.

"The Joy of the Just"

Before its original publication in the *American Poetry Review* (July–August 1974), "The Joy of the Just" had already enjoyed a lengthy existence among Gardner's unpublished drafts. Perhaps the earliest form of the story preserved in the Gardner collection at the University of Rochester appears as pages 145–82 of a typed manuscript of *Nickel Mountain* (box B-3). When Gardner cut this chapter from his novel he

changed the title, the setting, and the names of the characters; otherwise, he made few, if any, changes in plot and few revisions of any
kind, other than occasional changes and additions in phrasing early in
the story. The setting was originally in rural New York, and the drafts
reveal two rejected early titles: "Vengeance Is Aunt Rill's" and "Vengeance Is Aunt Anna's," reflecting early names for the central character, who became Aunt Ella Reikert in the final version. Similarly, the
characters Leon and Darthamae were originally the *Nickel Mountain*
characters Henry Soames and Callie.

Like "The Library Horror," this story concerns justice. Here, however, justice is conceived and executed entirely in the "real" world of
rural southern Illinois; the world of art does not intrude in any of its
official guises (music, dance, painting, literature), as it does in all the
other stories in this collection except "Trumpeter" and "The Art of
Living." In this story, the art is to be found in Aunt Ella's attempts to
impose what she thinks of as a proper moral order on her life and the
lives of those around her.

Convinced that she has been run off the road by the preacher's wife
(an unlicensed driver), Aunt Ella is determined to have "justice"
against the preacher and his wife, who persistently deny that the wife
was driving. The preacher claims that he was driving and that Aunt
Ella was on the wrong side of the road. It appears that the preacher is
lying about who was driving, but it also seems likely that Ella, with
her poor eyesight, may have been driving on the wrong side of the
road. The situation, like many crucial situations in Gardner's fiction,
therefore remains ambiguous.

The plot of the story details Aunt Ella's increasingly outrageous
schemes to "do justice." As Morris observes and as Gardner's rejected
titles also suggest, her pursuit of justice quickly becomes confused
with a desire for vengeance and self-justification when no one believes
her version of the incident (Morris, 195). With the single-minded devotion and vast personal resources of a master artist, she uses the "old
gypsy pea trick" to convince the preacher that his expensive riding
horse is worthless and to swindle him out of the animal for fourteen
dollars. She sends the horse to the glue factory, but her satisfaction is
ruined by the congregation's decision to buy the preacher a new horse.

Her next scheme is to invite the preacher and his wife to her house
on a Sunday to participate in her grape harvest and making of grape
juice. She slips the preacher and his wife grape juice spiked with gin,

with the intention of discrediting the preacher by sending him to his evening services drunk. He never appears before the congregation that evening, however, since, in his drunkenness, he accidentally sets the church afire with a candelabrum before services begin. The church burns to the ground, and "justice" is thwarted a second time when it appears that the preacher will get the new brick church he has been wanting after all.

Aunt Ella finally gets her justice, or revenge, the next day when the preacher returns to her house for his car. She has backed the car fifteen feet down her driveway, planted the preacher's wife's hat beside the driver's-side door, and lain down a few feet behind the car, pretending to be dead. As intended, the preacher assumes that his wife has run over Aunt Ella. He tries to cover for her, explaining to the deputy that he was driving and "never knew she was there till I felt the bump" (*AL*, 134). There was no "bump," of course, and Aunt Ella is unhurt. The preacher is severely discomfited and embarrassed before a small congregation, at least, and Aunt Ella achieves some measure of satisfaction. She insists to the end that her motive "wasn't wrath": "I did it for his correction, out of pure charity. Bless him" (*AL*, 135).

The spirit of this story, in spite of the potentially dire effects of Aunt Ella's quest for justice and some touches of meanness in both her character and the preacher's, is essentially comic. Everyone lives through it, and the preacher will probably be a better person as a result of his ordeal. Moreover, all the characters are more or less attractive. Like virtually all Gardner's characters, they are lovingly and sympathetically drawn; there are no real villains.

Something is amiss, however. A handwritten note on a manuscript page in the Gardner Papers (box B-3) indicates that Gardner at one point in the story's evolution thought of its theme as "faith vs. works." Gardner often remarked that artistic affirmation ultimately involves an act of faith, and it may be that Aunt Ella, in her maniacally determined and undeniably artful works, is deficient in faith. (Ironically, she complains after the horse-swindling incident that the preacher has insurance: "Now you tell me, Leon James, would a man that trusted in the Lord go out buying *in*surance?") Not content merely to affirm the universe by her art, she insists, like Luther Flint in "The King's Indian," on compelling the universe, and she very nearly does serious harm by her machinations. Though no nihilist or anarchist, she is nevertheless a flawed practitioner of the art of living.

"Vlemk the Box-Painter"

By far the longest story in the collection, "Vlemk the Box-Painter" was one of the stories frequently singled out by reviewers for special comment. As usual, that commentary was mixed. Bruce Allen, for example, called "Vlemk" "an interminable allegory," and Sam Coale, a critic generally sympathetic to Gardner's fiction, classed it among his least successful works. Similarly, Julian Moynahan identified "Vlemk" as the "worst" story in the collection, and various other reviewers branded the story as overlong, contrived, and preachy. On the other hand, Edmund Fuller found "Vlemk" the best of the stories, a "rich fairy tale for grown-ups," and Roger Harris placed it among the best of Gardner's works. Anne Tyler went so far as to call it "a masterpiece."[36] One of the most judicious reviewers, Ursula Le Guin, herself a talented writer of fiction, found "Vlemk" seriously flawed by Gardner's failure to maintain the integrity of his "fabulous" world; he deliberately introduced anachronisms to which she objected. Le Guin, incidentally, was reviewing the original publication of *Vlemk* as a separate book, which she considered along with the novel *Freddy's Book*. Unlike most reviewers, she had high praise for the latter (see Morace, 163, 175).

In some respects, the complaints of several reviewers seem justified. The story is long, and even a sympathetic reader who generally enjoys Gardner's fiction may find that the narrative drags occasionally. Moreover, readers who are familiar with the arguments for the moral impact of art that Gardner had recently advanced in *On Moral Fiction* and who have observed the thematic importance of the influence of art on life in the other stories in *The Art of Living* may well sense that "Vlemk" is to some degree "contrived" to illustrate the validity of the author's philosophical position. Such a perception, I believe, would be accurate.

The critical question such authorial manipulation raises has to do with the degree to which the story is flawed by it. The story is an allegory, certainly, and one that lacks even the decent camouflage of a realistic setting and characters. Allegories of this type (one thinks of *Piers Plowman* and Bunyan's *Pilgrim's Progress*, to name two extreme examples) have always been contrived to validate their author's beliefs, and given Gardner's knowledge of and propensity for imitating the forms of archaic fiction, it should perhaps not be surprising that he would write a story of this type. One problem may be that such writing, especially when it is obvious or heavy-handed, as "Vlemk" tends to be in spots, does not enjoy the favor of modern critical taste. Another, perhaps more serious objection is that, to the extent that "Vlemk" is actually "programmed" by the author to validate previously held beliefs, the story would seem to violate Gardner's often-repeated insistence that writing fiction is a process during which the author discovers what his beliefs are. In *On Moral Fiction* and elsewhere, Gardner roundly condemned fiction that starts with fixed beliefs and then manipulates plot and character to support them.

On the other hand, some reviewers, as we have seen, were quite charmed by "Vlemk" and thought it an excellent story. In some ways this too is an accurate perception. Aside from the obtrusiveness of the allegory, the writing is masterly, as usual. Gardner manages the complex plot with customary skill, and the scenes are splendidly realized, rich in authenticating detail. Most importantly, perhaps, the characters are drawn with such sympathy and depth that readers not rendered hostile by the allegorical and fabulous nature of the story may find themselves caring as much for the characters as the author apparently did. In this respect Gardner's characters differ markedly from the stick figures drawn by Bunyan or the author of *Piers Plowman* and approximate the rich humanity of, say, Chaucer's allegorical characters.

A test of Gardner's achievement in drawing character in this story may be the reader's reaction to the talking portrait of the princess. When the "real" princess imposes upon Vlemk the task of painting a portrait of her so real that it can actually speak as a condition for further discussion of marriage, Vlemk does just that. The portrait, done on a small box, not only speaks but becomes a major character in the story. Though immobile, the portrait has thoughts and feelings, and through its conversations with Vlemk (upon whom the portrait has put a curse, so that he cannot speak) we come to know the portrait in the same way we know the other characters. Thus Gardner imposed upon himself a task analogous to that imposed by the princess upon Vlemk: to turn a picture on a wooden box into a character readers can sympathize with and care about. It seems to me that he was successful.

Regardless of whether Gardner forced the plot to fit preconceived beliefs, the meaning of the allegory is familiar to anyone who has read the preceding seven stories in *The Art of Living*: art influences life. In a situation that recalls the central device of Oscar Wilde's *Picture of Dorian Gray* (and ultimately reverses it, when the portrait causes the physical and mental health of the princess to deteriorate), the portrait of the princess contains hints of flaws or imperfections in her character.

Vlemk later extracts these faults and focuses on them in a series of additional portraits, which he thinks of as "reality boxes." These portraits, which do not speak, have such titles as "The Dream of Debauchery," "The Princess Looking Bored," "The Princess Considers Revenge," "The Queen Full of Pride" (after the death of her father, when the princess becomes queen), and "The Queen Envious." By introducing these portraits, Gardner incidentally imitates another convention of the medieval allegory, that of the pageant of the Seven Deadly Sins, to which he adds "Despair" and "Madness" and presumably one other.

After the queen sees these other portraits, "ten obscene masks of corruption," she eventually becomes convinced that they reflect her essential nature. She loses the will to live and declines into a condition like that depicted in the portrait Vlemk calls "The Princess Almost Dead of Despair." She is saved when Vlemk attempts to remove the "imperfections" in the original portrait and takes the improved version to the palace. The queen, apparently on her deathbed, "come[s] up to the standard" of the new portrait, realizing that she has "become exactly like the picture on the box," and is redeemed. The prince, heretofore an amazingly inept and stupid character, explains that Vlemk, in retouching the original portrait, had "painted what you *thought* was a picture of perfection, but it came out exactly as it had been before you started!" (*AL*, 238–39). The portrait thus seems to represent that reconciliation between the real and the ideal—a simultaneous affirmation of both—wherein Gardner repeatedly insists the redemptive power of true art lies.

The principal import of the story, the message that life reflects and imitates art, is more clearly recapitulated in the situation of one of the minor characters. In a shameless ploy to obtain free drinks, Vlemk paints a flattering portrait of the "fat, sullen barmaid" and gives it to her. In the portrait, Vlemk had "given the barmaid a childlike smile" and "the eyes of a twelve-year-old milkmaid," and has "reddened her chin and removed certain blemishes, turning others . . . to beauty marks. He'd lifted her breasts a little, and tightened her skin, raised a sagging eyebrow, increased the visibility of her dimple. In short, he'd made her beautiful."

Vlemk gets his free drinks, and before long, a "curious thing" begins to happen to the barmaid: "She became increasingly similar to the fraudulent painting, smiling as she served her customers, looking at strangers with the eyes of an innocent, standing so erect, in her foolish pride, that her breasts were almost exactly where Vlemk had painted them" (*AL*, 160–61). As her self-image grows more like that suggested by the painting, the barmaid's life improves as well. She rises out of her sullenness, degradation, and after-hours prostitution to the extent that, before the story ends, she is engaged to be married and well on her way to respectability and, perhaps, happiness.

"Come on Back"

As most reviewers who commented specifically on this story noted with approval, "Come on Back" is written in the "rural-realistic" vein that Gardner had mined in *Nickel Mountain* and *October Light*, as well as in stories like "Redemption" and "The Joy of the Just." The story is closest to "Redemption" in that it is apparently based on Gardner's memories of his childhood and family in western New York State. Although Gardner changes the name of his mother's side of the family from Jones to Hughes and never mentions his father's family name, it is clear enough that the narrator, who in this reminiscence is nicknamed Buddy (Gardner's childhood family nickname), is Gardner himself.

Concerning "Redemption," Howell has shown how Gardner altered certain autobiographical facts to suit his artistic purposes (Howell, 1985, 3–6), and it seems not unlikely that he made comparable changes in "Come on Back." At any rate, Gardner apparently did not rely entirely on his memories in reconstructing the setting in Remsen, New York. Among the books from Gardner's office and study preserved in the Rochester collection is one entitled *A Narrative History of Remsen, New York*, by Millard F. Roberts (box B-2). A few marginal notes in Gardner's hand show that he examined the book, and the opening sentence of "Come on Back" mentions that Remsen was formerly called Jack and that "nearly all the people who lived there were Welsh" (*AL*, 145). Similarly, Roberts's book begins with a discussion of the old name, explaining it as a Welsh pronunciation of the name *Jake*. Gardner may have used other details from this source, but the debt does not appear to be extensive.

"Come on Back" renders the narrator's childhood memories of family visits to the household of his maternal great-uncle in Remsen. The household consists of Uncle Ed, who owns a feed mill; his wife, the narrator's Aunt Kate; and Ed's brother, Uncle Charley, who works at the feed mill for a small salary and lives in a basement room of Ed's house. The story centers on the narrator's memories of Uncle Charley and his fate.

The usual occasions for visits to Remsen are the Welsh singing festivals, particularly one called the Cymanfa Ganu, which, as Charley explains to the narrator, "means 'Come on Back' . . . 'Come on back to Wales,' that is. That's what all the Welshmen want, or so they think" (*AL*, 264).

The singing festival becomes the turning point of the story, as it is also of Charley's life. Uncle Charley is peculiar, all his life the family member of his generation "who'd been of no account." He never married, "never found a good woman, *that's* what's wrong with him," the narrator remembers his grandmother telling him. But it was more than that. In his younger days, Charley had possessed a "wonderful tenor voice" and "wouldn't have missed a Cymanfa Ganu or an Eisteddfod— the really big sing, where hundreds and hundreds of Welshmen came together."

It was Charley's voice that was his "downfall," the narrator remembers overhearing his grandmother say. "It gave him ideas." Later, Buddy asks his grandmother what she meant by those remarks. Her answer is the key to the story's meaning. "Well," she says, "Singing's got its place. But a body can get to thinking, when he's singing with a choir, that that's how the whole blessed world should be, and then when he comes down out of the clouds it's a terrible disappointment." Along with "a good woman," Charley needed "bills to pay, whippersnappers—*that'll* bring you down from your *la-la-la*," the grandmother says (*AL*, 250).

On one of Buddy's visits to Remsen, Charley takes "a tumble" at the feed mill and suffers a badly broken leg. The following summer, at the next visit, Charley's leg has healed, but the rest of him has not. He is a changed man, feebler and more frail than before, unable to do his former work and noticeably gloomier in outlook. But it is time for the Cymanfa Ganu, and this year for the first time, Buddy will be allowed to attend.

The event is held in an old wooden church, crowded to bursting. Buddy is wedged between his father and Uncle Charley, standing on his chair, when, "like a shock of thunder that made the whole room shake, they began to sing":

> They sang, as Welsh choruses always do, in numerous parts, each as
> clearly defined as cold, individual currents in a wide, bright river.

There were no weak voices, though some, like Uncle Charley's, were reedy and harsh—not that it mattered; the river of sound could use it all. They sang as if the music were singing itself through them—sang out boldly, no uncertainties or hesitations; and I, as if by magic, sang with them, as sure of myself every note of the way as the wisest and heartiest in the room. Though I was astonished by my powers, I know, thinking back, that it was not as miraculous as I imagined. Borne along by those powerful voices, the music's ancient structure, only a very good musician could have sung off key. And yet it did seem miraculous. It seemed our bones and blood that sang, all heaven and earth singing harmony lines, and when the music broke off on the final chord, the echo that rang on the walls around us was like a roaring Amen. (*AL*, 266)

Like the moment when the music "lifts off" in "Nimram," this represents yet another occurrence of the "artistic moment" that unites "all heaven and earth," when the real and the ideal are momentarily reconciled by art. In the narrator's memory, the experience is distinctly mystical: "We were outside ourselves, caught up in a *hwell*, as the Welsh say. It really did seem to me, once or twice, that I looked down on all the congregation from the beams above our heads" (*AL*, 267). Uncle Charley, though not Buddy's father or Uncle Ed, weeps, tears streaming "from his brown eye and blue eye, washing his cheeks, dripping from his moustache, making his whole face shine," and so do several of the women. After the event, Ed pronounces it a "good sing," and Buddy's father notes the "good turn-out." Uncle Charley remains ominously silent.

The next evening, Charley does not come in for supper. Hours later, his body is found in the creek across the road, behind the blacksmith's shop, where he has drowned himself. Charley's fatal depression is reminiscent of the situations of certain characters in "The Warden," although it does not seem to reproduce any one of them exactly. He is perhaps most like the anarchist Mallin, who hates the real because it falls short of the ideal, but instead of attacking the real as Mallin does—going at the universe with dynamite—Charley, like the warden, turns his disappointment against himself. Gardner thus finds (or creates), in an apparently autobiographical situation, an analogue or exemplification of the situation he presented fabulistically in "The Warden." Uncle Charley is ultimately unable to reconcile the real and the ideal, or to accept the disparity between them.

"Come on Back" ends on an affirmative note, however. In the assembly of friends and neighbors in Ed's living room the following night, there is the predictable talk of what a fine singer Charley had been, how he would be missed at the festivals, and so on, as well as other talk of crops, weather, politics, marriages. But eventually "the whole conversation died out like embers in a fireplace, and as the stillness deepened, settling in like winter or an old magic spell, it began to seem that the silence was unbreakable, our final say."

The silence is redeemed when "an old farmer named Sy Thomas, sitting in the corner with his hands folded, twine around his pants cuffs, cleared his throat, pushed his chin out, face reddening, eyes evasive, and began to sing" (*AL*, 269). The others gradually join in, and although the scene is brief and understated, it is clearly a reprise of the artistic moment. Humanity is again united against darkness and despair, penetrating the ideal from a base in the real, by the magic of art.

"The Art of Living"

Strategically placed at the end, the title story in *The Art of Living* is one of Gardner's finest and most representative fictions. Its virtues include well-drawn, fascinating characters—chiefly the narrator, Finnegan, and the cook, Arnold Deller, though the minor characters are convincing as well—and a sustained narrative interest that creates in the reader's mind the "vivid and continuous dream" Gardner repeatedly insisted good fiction should be. Moreover, the sense of time (during the Vietnam War, with all the contradictions and conflicts it spawned in the American mind) and the setting (an unnamed town in New York) are evoked by passages rich in description and authenticating detail. In these respects "The Art of Living" is as superbly crafted as anything Gardner wrote.

Reviewers who commented directly on this story were, as usual, divided between praise and scorn (see Morace, 186–98). Among the detractors were several who, apparently operating upon assumptions curiously foreign to the critical evaluation of literature, found the story's central event (the stealing, slaughtering, cooking, and eating of a dog) "outrageous," "gruesome," and "shocking," as well as a few who thought Arnold Deller's ranting diatribes a thin mask for the author's didactic doctrines. The later, more deliberate and thoughtful analyses of Cowart and Morris appraise the story more accurately and more favorably.

Thematically, as Cowart observes, "The Art of Living" "recapitu-lat[es] . . . the subjects of the preceding stories," including "death, insanity, war, and the desire for revenge," and poses the question, "How . . . can art help man deal with the kind of senseless, unjust violence the world does to him?" (Cowart, 184). In this story, however, the "art" in question is not music, dance, painting, or "justice"; it is the art implied by the title, specifically embodied in the everyday, utterly mundane, and universal human activity of cooking.

Arnold Deller, the middle-aged cook at Dellapicallo's Restaurant, father of three young girls and a son, Rinehart, recently killed in Viet-nam, lectures members of the local motorcycle gang, the Scavengers, who "hang out" at the restaurant. The Scavengers, including the nar-rator, Finnegan, are a far cry from Hell's Angels. They are "really just a bunch of greaser kids in second-hand black jackets, fighting pimples, hanging around, waiting to get drafted and shot at," living somewhere between the kids who joined the marines as soon as possible and those who went to college "to get out of it" (*AL*, 275). They haunt the res-taurant during afternoons, tolerating Arnold's rant for the pleasure of observing the owner's granddaughter, Angelina, who works there after school.

Arnold harangues the Scavengers, especially Finnegan, in whom he apparently senses a more receptive intelligence than in the others, on the subject of the evolution of human love and community. Inveighing against their aimlessness, he argues that a person must have "some kind of center to his life, some one thing he's good at that other people need from him, like, for instance, shoemaking. I mean something or-dinary but at the same time holy, if you know what I mean. Very spe-cial. Something *ritual*—like, better yet, cooking!" (*AL*, 282).

The lesson in this is that human beings are not just animals, living purely by instinct, but creatures who must "think things out, under-stand our human nature, figure out how to become what we are." Ar-nold then traces the evolution of human love, and the human "war instinct," from the human necessity to protect the young of the species for ten or twelve years following birth. The babies that survive are mostly those with parents who are "the best at holding grudges, the ones that are *implacable*." While this situation fosters love of children, then relatives, then neighbors, then "dead relatives and whatever bits of wisdom they may have scratched on pieces of wood or stone before they died," it also fosters absolute hatred of "the enemy, the stranger." Such behavior is fine, Arnold argues, as long as people "stay in tight little groups." But when Italians and Irish, or Welsh, Germans, Jews, Asians, and blacks try to live in the same town, "we've gotta expand our horizons, retrain our instincts a little," Arnold maintains. "That's when you've gotta use your head—you see? Love by policy, not just instinct. That's the Art of Living. Not just instinct; something you do on purpose. Art!" (*AL*, 285–86).

Arnold goes on to explain that art, as a center of order, evokes universal human emotions that people "can get together on." The ultimate effect of art, "what it's all about," he says, is "making life startling and interesting again, bringing families together, or lovers, what-not." He has used as an example of such a communal affair a "certain dish" that his son, Rinehart, had eaten "over there in Asia" and had written him about. It had been "a dish you might think no American would touch, given our prejudices. But it was made so perfectly, it was so downright outstanding, sooner or later you just had to give in to it. That's what he wrote. I've got the letter. It wasn't just food, it was an *occasion*. It was one of the oldest dishes known in Asia. Sit down to that dinner—this is what he wrote, and he was right, dead right—you could imagine you were eating with the earliest wisemen in the world" (*AL*, 287).

Evidently Arnold has spoken of this matter before. Angelina's father, Joe the bartender, has overheard Arnold's discourse and interrupts: "'No!' he shouted, apparently at Arnold. 'I don't give a damn about all your crazy talk. *No, black, dog!*'" (*AL*, 289).

The Scavengers leave the restaurant to cruise on their bikes, but later in the evening Angelina visits Finnegan in his garage. She wants his help in obtaining a "completely black dog" so that Arnold can cook, from an "ancient Chinese recipe" he has found, a dish called "Imperial Dog." "According to the book," she says, "it's supposed to be the absolutely most elegant dish in the world," and it "has to be killed just a minute before it's cooked" (*AL*, 297).

Finnegan objects but eventually agrees to "round up the gang" and try to acquire the necessary black dog, partly because he is infatuated with Angelina and partly because he realizes, as Angelina does, that Arnold is compelled to cook this dish in memory of his dead son. He also understands that Angelina is not doing this "only to oppose her father's power": "Maybe it had to do with Rinehart, how he'd carried her around on his shoulders when she was five and he was nine; had to do with Arnold Deller's immense, exasperating sorrow" (*AL*, 300).

Unable to bring themselves to kidnap some child's pet, the Scavengers break into a pet shop, steal a black dog of indeterminate breed, and deliver it to the restaurant after midnight.

The restaurant is closed, inhabited only by Arnold and his assistant (Ellis, a boy of Italian and American Indian ancestry), Angelina and her father, and the Scavengers. Arnold proceeds with the gory business of preparing Imperial Dog despite Joe's opposition. When Arnold defies him, Joe calls his father, the owner, old man Dellapicallo. But Arnold has a deal with the old man: he can prepare anything he wishes as a "chef's special," as long as he finds someone to eat it. When the old man arrives, things take a serious turn. If Arnold does not find customers to feed his dish to, he will be fired.

Arnold continues his preparations, raving about the shoddiness and artificiality of modern life, especially in regard to food (tasteless, trucker tomatoes, "the packaged, drugged-up meat at your supermarket") and the war ("Pentagon budgets in the multi-multi-billions" and "airplanes dropping bombs from so high up they don't know there's people down there"). Inevitably, his rant turns to the subject of art:

> Arnold was raving, "I'm an artist, you understand that? What's an artist? How's he different from an *ordinary* nut? An artist is a man who makes a covenant with tradition. Not just dreams, grand hopes and abstractions—no, *hell* no—a covenant with something that's *there*, pots and paintings, recipes: the specific that makes things indefinite come alive—assuming you don't get lost in 'em, the specifics, I mean. Salt, for instance. A man can get lost in the idea of salt— too much, too little, what the ancients thought of it, whether you should shake it with the left hand or the right—No! *That's* not art! *Dead* art! *Cancel!*" He gasped, jumped in again, swinging his left arm in front of him as if driving back hordes. "The artist's contract is, come hell or high water he won't go cheap, he'll never quit trying for the best. Maybe he fails, maybe he sells out and hates himself. You know it can happen just like you know you can stop loving your wife, but all the same you make the promise. Otherwise you have to go with ordinary craziness, which is disgusting." He spit. Forgot himself and spit right on the floor. (*AL*, 305–6)

Reviewers who objected that Gardner made the cook his mouthpiece in "The Art of Living" undoubtedly had passages like this one in mind. Certainly they were correct in identifying these remarks as reflections of the author's beliefs about art, but they were wrong in thinking of the speaker as a mere puppet. Arnold Deller is his own character, and he presents his conclusions in his own terms. They are drawn from his own experiences and thought processes, not Gardner's. What they reveal is a character who, by his own unique route, has arrived at essentially the same conclusions about art as Gardner.

As the time passes 3:00 A.M. and the Imperial Dog nears doneness, other guests arrive: Arnold's three daughters, ages ten to eighteen, who have come to check on their father. The meal that ensues becomes a sacrament, as Cowart points out, "with overtones of Passover and the Christian Eucharist. The dog they consume is a symbol of the sacrificed Rinehart, whose name derives from *rein Herz*, 'pure heart.' Those present number eleven: the cook, the cook's helper, old man Dellapicallo, and the eight boys and girls. The manager [bartender, actually], who refuses to partake and walks off, is the Judas who rounds out the apostolic twelve" (Cowart, 186).

Finnegan feels sorry for Joe, who departs in defeat, thinking that Joe "was the one who'd been right—sane and civilized from the beginning." But Joe's sanity and civilization are not in themselves sufficient to enable him to participate in the sacrament of art. Finnegan also notes that, as he left, Joe's "walk was oddly mechanical, and the way he shook his head when he looked back at us from the door, it was as if under his hair he had springs and gears" (*AL*, 309). Like the automaton replacement for the murdered Captain Dirge devised by Luther Flint (or Wilkins) in "The King's Indian," Joe is incapable of a fully human response.

Those who remain to partake represent a diverse ethnic and national mixture: the Germanic Arnold and his daughters; Arnold's assistant Ellis, half-Indian and half-Italian; Finnegan, who is half-Irish; Angelina and two of the Scavengers, Tony and Lenny, who are Italian; and the other Scavenger, Benny Russo, whose name suggests a Russian or possibly French background. The other side of the world is represented by the "thousands and thousands of dead Asians" whose invisible presence, along with Rinehart's, the diners sense in the darkness beyond the candlelight.

Symbolically, the meal unites humanity in a sacramental act of love and art. The diners physically present are the "distinguished representatives of all who couldn't make it this evening, the dead and the unborn" (*AL*, 310). This final scene thus takes its place with other convocations of "ghosts"—the dead and the unborn—in Gardner's fic-

tion, notably those in *Nickel Mountain* and *Mickelsson's Ghosts*, but re-
calling as well the evocation of "the breathless dead of the whole
world's history" and "all of humanity, living and dead . . . come together for one grand onslaught" as the music lifts off in "Nimram."
Such scenes, including this one, represent the holy communion of all
humankind—past, present, and future—that Gardner believed to be
the highest achievement of art.

"Julius Caesar and the Werewolf"

The only one of Gardner's stories to be published after his death, "Julius Caesar and the Werewolf" appeared in the September 1984 issue of *Playboy* magazine. According to the editor's note, Gardner "had just begun to make minor revisions" in the story at the time of his fatal motorcycle accident on 14 September 1982. From the evidence in the Gardner collection at Rochester, it appears that "Julius Caesar and the Werewolf" may well have been the last short story Gardner worked on. A typed draft of the story carries the note "first try—abandoned at once, March 15, 82," and another, undated draft is labeled "2nd try" (box B-14). It is interesting, though perhaps purely coincidental, that the first draft is dated on the anniversary of Julius Caesar's assassination.

This story is unusual among Gardner's fictions in that it does not directly or overtly concern the relations of art with society and life. Nevertheless, its subject, Julius Caesar, was an author of considerable note (his writings have been standard texts in Latin classes for centuries), as well as an accomplished student and practitioner of military and political "arts," and the narrator has studied his subject (also Julius Caesar) with as much care and devotion as any artist. Thematically and technically, the story is quintessentially Gardnerian.

In its epistolary narrative framework, however, "Julius Caesar and the Werewolf" is unique among Gardner's stories. Its form is that of a letter written by Caesar's elderly personal physician, presumably to an unnamed medical colleague. The early drafts indicate that Gardner originally intended to name the recipient; the letter was originally addressed to "Fabio" (crossed out), then to "Vitellius" (also crossed out), and then to "Febricius" (Gardner Papers, box B-14). Evidently, Gardner decided in a later revision to eliminate the addressee's name entirely. The letter is written in several installments, over a period of three or four days immediately preceding and following Caesar's assassination. The last installment, which recounts the assassination itself, is written shortly after the event, perhaps on the same day or the next day after.

The presumption that the intended recipient of the letter is a medical colleague is warranted by the narrator's discussion of and frequent references to medical matters that would be inappropriate if addressed to a layman. The letter presumes the recipient's familiarity with these matters. Moreover, there are numerous indications that the letter is written in part as a reply to the recipient's previous letter, in which he had inquired about certain symptoms and reports of erratic behavior on Caesar's part.

The narrator confirms that, indeed, Caesar has exhibited some definitely "odd" behavior of late, but he does not regard the symptoms as cause for alarm: "The symptoms you mention," he writes, "are, indeed, visible, though perhaps a little theatricized by your informant." The symptoms include "nervous attacks, sudden tempers, funks and so forth," but Caesar has always been subject to these, the narrator writes, citing his thirty-five years (since the Gallic campaigns) of close observation as Caesar's physician ("JCW," 74). In a later installment, we learn of some stranger manifestations.

The central event of the story, perhaps surprisingly, is not the assassination; that mighty deed is tacked on in haste at the end, almost as a postscript. Instead, the narrator offers, as a possible explanation of "this change [in Caesar] you inquire of and find so disturbing," to recount the strange occurrences of "[s]ome days ago, March first." The narrator has "a guess I might offer, but it's so crackpot I think I'd rather sit on it." He will describe the situation and allow his correspondent to "draw [his] own conclusions" ("JCW," 78).

On the evening of 1 March, Caesar summoned the narrator to examine the horribly mutilated body of a young man who had apparently been torn apart by wolves. Similar incidents have been occurring for months, Caesar explains, but this time his soldiers have captured a young woman trying to hide the body. The young woman, under questioning, says that the "wolf" was actually a man. The woman, or girl, no more than sixteen, leads Caesar, the narrator, and three soldiers to her father's apartment in a Roman slum. Her father, it turns out, is a werewolf—at the moment in human form, because the full moon is tombed in clouds, but in a stuporous condition and unable to speak coherently. Caesar questions the werewolf intently, asking, "What does it feel like, coming on?" When the werewolf is unable to answer, Caesar says, "Never mind that. What does it feel like afterward?" Again there is no answer, and Caesar finally asks, "Tell me this: How many people have you killed?" The werewolf ventures two tentative answers: "Hundreds?" "Thousands?" ("JCW," 176). The werewolf rambles incoherently for a while longer, but then the clouds part and the room fills with moonlight. The man is transformed into a wolf and springs, causing Caesar to kill the creature with his sword, as the girl, who has perhaps also turned into a wolf, runs out the door on all fours and vanishes.

It is apparently from this bizarre episode that the narrator dates the increased "oddity" in Caesar's behavior, but he cannot quite pin down a diagnosis: "One cannot call it mania in any usual sense—delusional insanity, dementia, melancholia, and so forth. Nonetheless, he's grown odd. (No real cause for alarm, I think.)" The narrator cites the "squall of honors" recently conferred on Caesar: "statues, odes, feasts, gold medals, outlandish titles: Prince of the Moon, Father of Animals, Shepherd of Ethiopia and worse—more of them every day." The problem is that nearly all these tributes are Caesar's own inventions, "insinuated into the ears of friendly senators or enemies who dare not cross him," and Caesar seems "delighted," laughing, "not cynically but with childlike pleasure" at "each new outrage he conceives or hears suggested," "as if astonished by how much foolishness the gods will put up with." Indeed, Caesar seems to have taken an unwonted interest in religion, even to the point of "reasoning with priests." The narrator is unwilling to attribute this behavior to megalomania but does cite one instance of what "seemed authentic lunacy": he overheard Caesar talking to the carp and goldfish in the aquarium, telling them to "straighten up those ranks, there! Order! Order!" and shaking his finger at them. On another occasion he found Caesar "hunkered down, earnestly reasoning—so it seemed—with a colony of ants" ("JCW," 178). Oddest of all, the narrator writes, is Caesar's recent proposal to conduct a war against Persia.

The rest is denouement. The omens come: exploding stars, discord in the heavens. And visitors to the palace darkly urge Caesar to avoid the forum the next day. Clearly, a plot is afoot. But Caesar goes to the forum, and the assassination proceeds as planned. The narrator records it clinically, focusing on the amazing strength Caesar showed, lunging about, hurling senators off him though spurting blood from a hundred wounds, and so on.

In attempting to sort out what all this means, it seems best to consider Gardner's sources. Much of the background, other than the character of the narrator, derives from Plutarch's account of the life of Julius Caesar. Characteristically, however, Gardner has taken mere hints in

Plutarch and amplified and expanded them, fleshing them out with such detail that they seem real and authentic by modern fictional standards. Gardner had done much the same thing, on a larger scale, in his adaptations of Appollonius' *Argonautica* and Euripides' *Medea* in the epic *Jason and Medeia*. Instances in this story include Caesar's headaches and "falling sickness" (epilepsy), as well as the treatment of the assassination.

A more important source (or model) for this story, however, is Browning's remarkable epistolary poem "An Epistle: Containing the Strange Medical Experience of Karshish, the Arab Physician." Just as he had found in Browning's "Soliloquy of the Spanish Cloister" the inspiration for "The Temptation of St. Ivo," Gardner here returns to Browning's dramatic poetry and comes away with a much closer model for "Julius Caesar and the Werewolf." At first glance, Browning's poem and Gardner's story may not seem closely related. I believe, however, that careful analysis will support the hypothesis that Gardner deliberately appropriated the form and general outline of the poem, as well as some fairly specific details, as a kind of matrix for his story.

"Karshish," it will be recalled, is in the form of a letter written by the title character, who is traveling in Palestine, to his medical colleague (or perhaps former mentor; the poem is ambiguous on this point) Abib, who remains at home. The time is evidently about the middle of the first century A.D. As Karshish notes at the end of his elaborate salutation, this is the twenty-second time he has written Abib during his travels. He writes now from Bethany, which lies from Jerusalem (his next major destination) "scarce the distance thence / A man with plague-sores at the third degree / Runs till he drops down dead" (lines 36–38).

After some travel notes (he's been robbed and beaten twice, and one town "declared [him] for a spy") and talk of various medical observations (that the Jews have a "happier cure" for "falling sickness" than "our school wots of"; that "there's a spider here" used in the preparation of some medicine—but he declines to give the recipe, distrusting the "Syrian runagate" who will, perhaps, deliver the letter; that certain medicinal substances in Judea are of better quality than "our produce"; and so on), Karshish thinks of ending the letter but reconsiders and goes on, almost reluctantly, to discuss the matter that "set me off a-writing first of all."

To summarize, Karshish has encountered in Bethany a local man, Lazarus by name, who believes that many years ago he was revived from death by "a Nazarene physician of his tribe." Karshish has interviewed the man himself as well as "elders of his tribe" who "Led in their friend, obedient as a sheep, / To bear my inquisition." The bulk of Karshish's letter is devoted to his analysis of this strange medical case and his description of Lazarus' condition and symptoms. His medical opinion is that "'Tis but a case of mania—subinduced / By epilepsy, at the turning-point / Of trance prolonged unduly some three days," and that Lazarus was too suddenly snapped out of his deathlike trance "by the exhibition of some drug / Or spell, exorcisation, stroke of art / Unknown to me and which 'twere well to know" (lines 79–84). He theorizes that Lazarus' abrupt return to consciousness made a "clear house" of his mind so suddenly that the first impression it received was indelibly printed there. That impression was that he was dead—"(in fact they buried him)"—and was recalled to life by the "Nazarene physician" who "bade 'Rise,' and he did rise."

Still, certain details of Lazarus' condition and behavior puzzle Karshish. Physically, he is a model of perfect health, as though "he were made and put aside to show." Emotionally, he exhibits a childlike serenity and simplicity and a peculiar indifference to all matters of common worldly concern, paying attention only when Karshish speaks directly to him and otherwise folding his hands and "[w]atching the flies that buzzed." It is as if he has actually glimpsed another plane of existence and is now a creature of two worlds—physically in this one but mentally (or spiritually) in the other. Karshish speculates that even "Should his child sicken unto death—why look / For scarce abatement of his cheerfulness, / Or pretermission of his daily craft" (lines 159–60). Moreover, Karshish senses that Lazarus feels somehow at crosspurposes between the two worlds, perceiving the conflicting laws of both simultaneously: "'It should be' balked by 'here it cannot be'" (line 190).

Karshish acknowledges that it would have been preferable to consult "the sage himself, the Nazarene / Who wrought this cure" (lines 244–45), but alas, that "learned leech" died "in a tumult many years ago, / Accused,—our learning's fate,—of wizardry" (lines 248–49). The leech's death occurred, Karshish reports, "when the earthquake fell"–the earthquake that Karshish refers to as "(Prefiguring, as soon appeared, the loss / To occult learning in our lord the sage / Who lived there in the pyramid alone)" (lines 253–55).

The oddest aspect of the case, which Karshish reluctantly reports only for the sake of complete medical frankness between physicians, is that Lazarus is convinced that his "curer" was none other than "God himself / Creator and sustainer of the world, / That came and dwelt in flesh on it awhile!" (lines 268–70). Karshish is most doubtful of this claim, observing that "after all, our patient Lazarus / Is stark mad; should we count on what he says?" (lines 263–64). Nevertheless, the Arab physician is intrigued by the Christian notion of the incarnation of an "All-Loving" god, as he closes his letter urging Abib to consider the import of such a thing: "The very God! think, Abib; dost thou think? / So, the All-Great, were the All-Loving too— / So, through the thunder comes a human voice" (lines 304–6).

The broad similarities between this poem and Gardner's story are hard to miss. They include, most notably, the epistolary form of both and the fact that in each the persona who writes the letter is a physician writing to a colleague about a strange medical case. Perhaps of less significance, but nonetheless true, is the fact that the time setting of poem and story are within a century of each other, mid-first-century B.C. for the story and mid-first-century A.D. for the poem.

Much more striking and significant are the numerous correspondences of "plot" and detail between the two. Many of these instances, appropriately, appear as similarities between the "cases" of Caesar (and the werewolf, with whom Caesar to some extent identifies) and Lazarus. Gardner's narrator presents Caesar as in some sense a creature of two worlds. He is unique in the narrator's experience in the vigor of his "animal spirits" and in his "speed," both physical and mental: "His body, it seems to me, runs by nature at an accelerated tempo." The narrator wonders "if he may not have some unknown substance in common with the violent little flea." Caesar has always appeared to the narrator "singular to the point of freakishness," "taller than other men, curiously black-eyed and blond-headed, like two beings in one body" ("JCW," 74).

The suggestion that he is "two beings in one body" is strengthened by the narrator's description of Caesar's "falling sickness," or epilepsy. (Karshish "officially" [but not confidently] diagnosed Lazarus' case as "mania—subinduced / By epilepsy," we recall.) Caesar's physician describes his subject during a seizure as "not unconscious but in some way transformed, as if seized for the moment by the laws of a different set of gods. (I mean, of course, 'forces' or 'biological constraints')" ("JCW," 76). This description suggests a parallel both with the werewolf, who is literally two beings in one body, and with Lazarus, who operates by two different sets of laws. Moreover, both Karshish and Gardner's narrator consider mania in their diagnoses.

Another place where the story bumps against the poem is in its description of Caesar's behavior during the sickness and death of his daughter Julia, to which, the narrator says, some attribute the changes in Caesar. Although "filled with woe . . . when the sickness first invaded her" and most solicitous for her care, "when Julia died, he kissed her waxy forehead and left the room and, so far as one could see, that was that." Afterward, "he seemed much the same man he'd been, not just externally but also internally, so far as my science could reach" ("JCW," 78). This passage corresponds with Karshish's speculation that should Lazarus' "child sicken unto death," there would be "scarce abatement of his cheerfulness, / Or pretermission of his daily craft."

Yet another important correspondence is to be found in Caesar's behavior after his interview with the werewolf, from which the narrator dates the most "disturbing" changes. After that event, Caesar becomes distinctly Lazarus-like, as if he, too, has glimpsed another world, the existence of which reorders his assessment of the importance of the things of this world. Like Lazarus, he takes a "childlike pleasure" in trivial or foolish things—the "squall" of honors and outlandish titles conferred on him, for example—and loses his cynicism. Like Lazarus, who "eyes the world now as a child," "affects the very brutes and birds," and is most interested in "[w]atching the flies that buzzed," Caesar communes with carp, goldfish, and a colony of ants. As Lazarus patiently awaits "that same death which must restore his being / To equilibrium," Caesar serenely ignores multiple warnings of a plot against him and goes to the forum on the ides of March, as if he also aspired to a wholeness of being that death would bring. Caesar's new interest in religion, "always busy with the gods, ignoring necessities, reasoning with priests," also reflects Lazarus' otherworldly concerns.

The werewolf, in whom, judging by the nature and intensity of his questions, Caesar evidently perceives an analogue to his own dual nature, also reflects the condition of Lazarus. When Caesar sees him, the werewolf is in a stupor, almost oblivious to his surroundings. Karshish twice uses the word *stupor* in describing Lazarus' mental state. The werewolf, in his rambling incoherence, also appears to attribute his condition to "gods" and seems, like Lazarus and Caesar, to suffer the conflicting pulls of two different sets of laws. One moment he mumbles, "Thank . . . gods . . .unspeakable," and the next he cries out, "Vile!" ("JCW," 178).

One further correspondence among several that might be cited will confirm the remarkable indebtedness of Gardner's story to Browning's poem. "Karshish" ended with the narrator's speculations on what it might mean if the "All-Great" had a loving and human side to His nature, if "through the thunder comes a human voice." The story ends with a similar, though transmuted, image, as Gardner's narrator evokes his memory of Caesar's dying cries, "still in my ears, strangely bright, like a flourish of trumpets or Jovian laughter" ("JCW," 180). The trumpets suggest a triumph rather than defeat, and one senses powerfully that the divine laughter is human and loving rather than cynical and mocking.

Given Gardner's career-long thematic interest in "resurrection" (the title of his first published novel was *The Resurrection*) as a metaphor for personal redemption or "salvation," it was perhaps inevitable that he would be drawn to Browning's poem on the subject of a literal resurrection. He would also have been attracted by the poem's evocation of love as a transcendent principle in the universe. In *Jason and Medeia* Gardner had desribed love as just such a principle, calling it "the god at the heart of things, / dumb to the structured surface—high ruler of the rumbling dance / behind the Unnamable's dream" (352), and the supreme importance of human love is a thematic constant in Gardner's fiction. Another lure Gardner would have found irresistible is the prominence of the conflict between the real and the ideal implicit in Lazarus' condition, the "'It should be' balked by 'here it cannot be.'" It is a theme we have seen repeatedly in Gardner's short stories, and one that recurs frequently in all his fiction.

Given also Gardner's frequent method of appropriating other writers' works that he found attractive and using them as sources and models for his own works, it was perhaps equally inevitable that he would eventually get around to working "Karshish" into the fabric of his fiction. In doing so, he wrought what must be regarded as a characteristic transformation of his source, creating a new work wholly his own, yet fully grounded in literary tradition and communicating with its antecedents at many points. Like Cleon, the title-persona in another of Browning's epistolary poems, he has "entered into sympathy" with his predecessors, "running these into one soul" (lines 143–44) and participating in a dialogue among writers that spans many centuries.

Finally, one may say of "Julius Caesar and the Werewolf," Gardner's last story, that, like many of his works, it shines with meaning that transcends the literal limits of its characters and setting. Julius Caesar, a werewolf of sorts, despite his uniqueness becomes a model for all humanity. We are all werewolves, double beings in a single body, participating in both this world and another. To recognize that duality and reconcile it, as Caesar does on the eve of his assassination, is to attain a serenity that amounts, in Gardner's terms, to mundane salvation.

Notes to Part 1

1. David Cowart, *Arches and Light: The Fiction of John Gardner* (Carbondale: Southern Illinois University Press, 1983); hereafter cited parenthetically.

2. Gregory L. Morris, *A World of Order and Light: The Fiction of John Gardner* (Athens: University of Georgia Press, 1984); hereafter cited parenthetically.

3. *Jason and Medeia* (New York: Knopf, 1973); hereafter cited parenthetically as *JM*.

4. *The Art of Living and Other Stories* (New York: Knopf, 1981); hereafter cited parenthetically as *AL*.

5. It should be noted, however, that Morris does recognize that the stories in Gardner's first collection, *The King's Indian*, are "composed and grouped along definite lines of thought" and that the diverse stories "blend submissively into a large and more impressive whole" (117). Cowart also acknowledges the "subtle interrelation of story with story" in *The King's Indian*, suggesting that "only Joyce's *Dubliners* surpasses" Gardner's collection in this regard (76).

6. Charles Johnson, one of Gardner's former creative writing students at Southern Illinois University who went on to become a successful novelist and short story writer, allegorically represents his "apprenticeship" under Gardner in the title story of his collection *The Sorcerer's Apprentice: Tales and Conjurations* (New York: Atheneum, 1986). Raymond Carver, another of Gardner's highly successful former students, describes in his foreword to Gardner's posthumously published *On Becoming a Novelist* (New York: Harper & Row, 1983) what it was like to study creative writing with Gardner in the late 1950s at Chico State. Other testimonials to Gardner's inspiration, concern, and unstinting helpfulness, both as teacher and as editor, may be found in the special tributary supplement published in the Fall 1984 number of *MSS* (a journal founded and edited by Gardner) and in Hart Wegner's article "'Dear Hart, Dear Heorot': John Gardner as Editor" (in *Thor's Hammer: Essays on John Gardner*, ed. Jeff Henderson [Conway: University of Central Arkansas Press, 1985], 75–88).

7. *The King's Indian: Stories and Tales* (New York: Knopf, 1974); hereafter cited parenthetically as *KI*.

8. "Julius Caesar and the Werewolf," *Playboy*, September 1984, 74–78, 86, 174–80; hereafter cited parenthetically as "JCW."

9. *Dragon, Dragon and Other Tales* (New York: Knopf, 1975), *Gudgekin the Thistle Girl and Other Tales* (New York: Knopf, 1976), *The King of the Hummingbirds and Other Tales* (New York: Knopf, 1977); hereafter cited parenthetically as *DD*, *G*, and *H*, respectively.

10. Publication data on these stories, as well as on Gardner's earlier stories, are given in the Chronology and Bibliography of this volume.

11. Marshall L. Harvey, "Where Philosophy and Fiction Meet: An Interview with John Gardner," *Chicago Review* 29, No. 4 (Spring 1978): 80–81.

12. Summaries of forty-eight substantive reviews of *KI* in Morace's *John Gardner: An Annotated Secondary Bibliography* (New York: Garland, 1984), 104–112, indicate that thirty reviews were favorable, eight were unfavorable, and ten were mixed; Morace's bibliography is hereafter cited parenthetically.

13. These reviews and others are quoted and summarized in Morace, 104–112. Original publication data may be found in Morace and in the Bibliography of this volume.

14. In a handwritten note on a manuscript page of a draft copy of "Pastoral Care," Gardner suggests that Pick himself may be the barren or "fruitless" tree (Gardner Papers, box B-11; see note 19). Surely he is, and he will be "blasted" by subsequent events. Unlike the fig tree (which Jesus curses eternally—a "sentence of death," as Pick notes in his sermon), however, Pick has a potential for redemption or resurrection, which is realized (or at least begun) in the story's final scene.

15. The Gardner Papers collection at the University of Rochester contains evidence of at least some of the "research" Gardner did for this story, in the form of a letter (presumably answering a query by Gardner) from Gene Rudzewicz on the subject of cloning and several offprints of early biological treatises by Mendel, Lamarck, Darwin, and others.

16. While this identification may seem strange to some, it should be remembered that Gardner often cited the animated cartoons of Walt Disney (as well as comic books and cartoons in general) as influences on his work. In view of Gardner's lifelong practice of borrowing material from the widest-imaginable range of sources, both famous and obscure, it is not particularly unlikely that he would use such a model as Mortimer Snerd or Howdy Doody.

17. Gardner's double billing on the program was, of course, a result of his fame both as a novelist and short story writer and as a medieval scholar and critic. *October Light* had won the Book Critics Circle Award for Fiction for the previous year (1976), and Gardner's two books on Chaucer (*The Life and Times of Chaucer* and *The Poetry of Chaucer*), both of them controversial, as usual, had just been published.

18. James G. Murray, Review of *The King's Indian: Stories and Tales*, by John Gardner, *Critic* 33 (March 1975): 71–73; Keith Nelson, in *Masterplots Annual 1975*, ed. Frank N. Magill (Englewood Cliffs, N.J.: Salem Press, 1976), 164–66.

19. The John Gardner Papers, the University of Rochester Library, Department of Rare Books and Special Collections, Rochester, N.Y.; hereafter cited parenthetically by box number.

20. Ed Christian, "An Interview with John Gardner," *Prairie Schooner* 54 (Winter 1981): 76.

21. John Howell, who is probably the most knowledgeable authority on the ways Gardner composed his fiction, has remarked in private conversation that Gardner would sometimes draw up such an outline after he had finished writing the work, to make sure the story or novel "worked" as he had intended. Considering that this outline contains an ending Gardner cut from the final version of the story, however, it seems more likely that he made the outline before he was completely finished with the story. This particular outline is reproduced in part 2 of this book.

22. Gardner had effected the "rebirth" of the "illustrated novel for adults," as Howell puts it, with the publication of *Grendel* in 1971 (*John Gardner: A Bibliographical Profile* [Carbondale: Southern Illinois University Press, 1980], xviii; hereafter cited parenthetically). All of Gardner's subsequent novels, collections of short stories, and children's books were illustrated, by various artists using a variety of media, including line drawings, woodcuts, and photography.

23. As noted in Howell's chronology, Gardner spent part of 1971 on a sabbatical year abroad, mostly in London, where he worked on "among other things, a film about a psychic professor, written for Telly Savalas (never made), and *Jason and Medeia*" (Howell, 1980, xviii).

24. *On Moral Fiction* (New York: Basic Books, 1978), passim; hereafter cited parenthetically as *OMF*.

25. See, for example, Alison Payne's essay "Clown, Monster, Magician: The Purpose of Lunacy in John Gardner's Fiction," in *Thor's Hammer: Essays on John Gardner*, 157–66). Cowart and Morris also discuss Gardner's "lunatic" characters, including Queen Louisa.

26. *Freddy's Book* (New York: Knopf, 1980), 246.

27. For a list of such words in *Jason and Medeia*, see Jeff Henderson, "John Gardner's *Jason and Medeia*: The Resurrection of a Genre," *Papers on Language and Literature* 22, no. 1 (Winter 1986): 84–85, n.

28. *The Sunlight Dialogues* (New York: Knopf, 1972), 3–5.

29. Roni Natov and Geraldine DeLuca, "An Interview with John Gardner," *The Lion and the Unicorn* 2 (Spring 1978): 114.

30. For summaries of these and other reviews of the children's books, see Morace, 112–15, 126–28.

31. Geraldine DeLuca and Roni Natov, "Modern Moralities for Children: John Gardner's Children's Books," In *John Gardner: Critical Perspectives*, ed. Robert A. Morace and Kathryn Van Spanckeren (Carbondale: Southern Illinois University Press, 1982), 89, 93; excerpted in part 3 of this volume.

32. A striking instance of Gardner's including in an adult story material whose full significance he knew only a few readers would understand occurs in "The Warden," when a "fool" visits the narrator and tries to sell him a book. The opening sentence of the book identifies it as Sartre's *Being and Nothingness*, a basic existentialist text. Gardner later argued in an interview with James Harkness (summarized in Morace, 43) that it did not matter that some readers would miss the connection, since the story can be understood and appreciated on different levels.

33. For a detailed discussion of the biographical facts and Gardner's alterations of them in this story, see Howell's essay "The Wound and the Albatross: John Gardner's Apprenticeship" in *Thor's Hammer: Essays on John Gardner*, 1–16; hereafter cited parenthetically.

"Redemption," as Howell points out, is drawn—along with the next story in *AL*, "Stillness"—from an unfinished autobiographical novel entitled "Stillness" that Gardner had put aside and did not return to prior to his death. In their original forms, both stories were chapters in this novel. *Stillness* and the fragmentary novel *Shadows* were published together after Gardner's death, under the editorship of his literary executor, Nicholas Delbanco.

34. Johnson's story appears in his collection *The Sorcerer's Apprentice*. As previously noted, Johnson is a former writing student of Gardner's who freely acknowledges his debt and gratitude to his teacher. Although Johnson's story is in no pejorative sense derivative, I suspect that it was inspired in part by Gardner's rendition of dog consciousness in "Trumpeter."

35. See Morris's discussion, 193–95; excerpted in part 3 of this volume.

36. These reviews and others are quoted and summarized in Robert A. Morace, *John Gardner: An Annotated Secondary Bibliography* (New York: Garland, 1984), 186–98.

Part 2

THE WRITER

Introduction

The materials presented in part 2, some of them printed for the first time, have been selected on the basis of two criteria. First, I have chosen passages that reveal as much as possible of the author's theories and beliefs about his own creative processes and about artistic creation in general. Second, I have attempted to include materials that illuminate Gardner's methods and intentions in regard to particular works. The selections are representative of the author's mind and art as he expressed them in a variety of contexts, from the carefully reasoned theoretical presentation in *On Becoming a Novelist* to the more spontaneous remarks in interviews and personal letters. The last two selections show Gardner in the very process of working out the methods and meanings of his fiction. Taken as a whole, these documents dramatically illustrate the seriousness and depth of commitment Gardner brought to his work as a writer of fiction.

The excerpt from the posthumously published *On Becoming a Novelist* contains Gardner's fullest description of the "trance state" he regarded as the crucial element in the creative process. Clearly, Gardner believes that the "quality of strangeness" all great art possesses originates in a mental state to which all successful artists are more or less susceptible. His detailed description of this condition as he perceived it during his composition of *Grendel* is one of the most striking and compelling such statements in the history of literary theory.

Gardner's interview with Natov and DeLuca presents his most substantial commentary on his children's books, revealing his specific motives and intentions as well as his general theoretical assumptions about children's literature. His remarks show that he took his children's stories quite as seriously as his adult fiction, particularly in regard to their moral dimensions and the responsibility the author assumes in writing for any audience.

The undated "Letter to Burton [Weber]," written to a friend whose book on *Paradise Lost* Gardner had edited for the Southern Illinois University Press, is included for the light it sheds on "The King's Indian" and other stories. The letter also typifies the kind of high-powered literary commentary Gardner habitually (if not compulsively) dashed off in "unofficial" correspondence and casual conversation. Some two-thirds of the letter is printed here; the rest consists of a commentary on Mahler's symphonies, conducted at a level of musical sophistication comparable with that of the literary remarks.

The last two selections, "Outline for 'The Warden'" and "Commentary on 'The King's Indian,'" demonstrate the care with which Gardner worked out his intricate plots and the significance with which he invested even the smallest details of his stories. The "Outline" is a slightly edited transcript of a two-page, handwritten document Gardner produced at some point during his composition of "The Warden." The name *Malist* (instead of *Mallin*, as in the final published version) and certain other details (notably the "cut" ending, which does not appear in the published story) would seem to indicate a date for the outline sometime prior to the author's final revisions. My editing has consisted of incorporating Gardner's caret-marked insertions into the appropriate lines, deleting material he crossed out, regularizing capitalization and punctuation, and eliminating a few irrelevant or illegible marginal notations.

The "Commentary" is also a transcript of handwritten notes Gardner made at some point during his composition of "The King's Indian." I have followed the same editorial practices as with the "Warden" outline.

From *On Becoming a Novelist*

As for the quality of strangeness, it is hard to know what can be said. There can be no great art, according to the poet Coleridge, without a certain strangeness. Most readers will realize at once that he is right. There come moments in every great novel when we are startled by some development that is at once perfectly fitting and completely unexpected—for instance the late, surprising entrance of Svidrigailov in *Crime and Punishment,* Mr. Rochester's disguise in *Jane Eyre,* the rooftop scene in *Nicholas Nickleby,* Tommy's stumbling upon the funeral in *Seize the Day,* the recognition moment in *Emma,* or those moments we experience in many novels when the ordinary and the extraordinary briefly interpenetrate, or things common suddenly show, if only for an instant, a different face. . . .

If I could explain exactly what I mean here, I could probably do what I think no one has ever done successfully: reveal the very roots of the creative process. The mystery is that even when one has experienced these moments, one finds, as mystics so often do, that after one has come out of them, one cannot say, or even clearly remember, what happened. In some apparently inexplicable way the mind opens up; one steps out of the world. One knows one was away because of the words on the page when one comes back, a scene or a few lines more vivid and curious than anything one is capable of writing—though there they stand. (That experience, I suspect, is the motivating impulse behind the many stories of unearthly experiences confirmed in the final paragraph by some ring or coin or pink ribbon left behind by the otherworldly intruder.) All writing requires at least some measure of trancelike state: the writer must summon out of nonexistence some character, some scene, and he must focus that imaginary scene in his mind until he sees it as vividly as, in another state, he would see the typewriter and cluttered desk in front of him, or last year's calendar on

Excerpted from *On Becoming a Novelist* by John Gardner (New York: Harper & Row, 1983), 56–61. © 1983 by the Estate of John Gardner. Reprinted by permission of Harper & Row Publishers, Inc.

the wall. But at times—for most of us, all too occasionally—something happens, a demon takes over, or nightmare swings in, and the imaginary *becomes the real*.

I remember that once, writing the last chapter of *Grendel*, this altered sense of things came over me with great force. It was not at the time a new or surprising experience; the one respect in which it was odd was that after I came out of it I seemed to remember vividly what had happened. Grendel has just had his arm torn off and recognizes that he will die. He has stubbornly insisted throughout the novel that we have no free will, that all life is brute mechanics, all poetic vision a cynical falsehood, and he clings even now to those opinions, partly for fear that optimism is cowardice, partly from stubborn self-love: even though Beowulf has banged Grendel's head against a wall, bullying him into making up a poem about walls, Grendel is hanging on for dear life to his convictions, in terror of being swallowed by the universe and convinced that his opinions and his identity are one and the same. The "inspired" passage (I am of course not talking about its aesthetic value) begins approximately here:

> No one follows me now. I stumble again and with my one weak arm
> I cling to the huge twisted roots of an oak. I look down past stars to
> a terrifying darkness. I seem to recognize the place, but it's impos-
> sible. "Accident," I whisper. I will fall. I seem to desire the fall, and
> though I fight it with all my will I know in advance that I can't win.
> Standing baffled, quaking with fear, three feet from the edge of a
> nightmare cliff, I find myself, incredibly, moving toward it. I look
> down, down, into bottomless blackness, feeling the dark power
> moving in me like an ocean current, some monster inside me, deep
> sea wonder, dread night monarch astir in his cave, moving me slowly
> to my voluntary tumble into death.

Throughout the novel I'd made occasional allusions to the poetry and prose of William Blake, a major influence on my ideas about the imagination (its power to transform and redeem). Here, when I was simply following Grendel in my imagination, trying to feel in myself what it might be like to flee through deep woods, bleeding to death, I suddenly fell, without having planned it, into what I can only describe as a powerful dream of a Blakean landscape: the huge twisted roots of the oak, then a dizzying reversal of up and down (I had the sense of Grendel as fallen onto his back, looking up past the tree but imagining he was looking down, an image that recalls my childhood fear that if the

planet is indeed round, I might one day fall off). Though the oak tree
is from Blake, it was tinged in my mind with other associations. In
Chaucer's poetry, with which I was then deeply involved, the oak is
associated with Christ's cross and with sorrow in general; by another
line it is associated with druids and human sacrifice, notions darkened
for me by my childhood reaction to songs like "The Old Rugged
Cross" (stained with blood so divine), grizzly and sickening reminders
of beheaded chickens, butchered cows, child thoughts of death with
undertones of guilt and the ultimate moral ugliness of God.

I did not, in my writing trance, separate these ideas out. I *saw*
Blake's tree, exactly the same tree I saw when I read Chaucer's *The
Book of the Duchess,* and its force was that of the cross I imagined in
childhood, messy with blood and gobbets of flesh (an unorthodox image, I realize). I think, though I'm not sure, that it was this sense of
the tree as tied to my childhood vision that made me react to it with a
sense of déjà vu. Imitating (in fact, feeling) Grendel's terror, I react in
Grendel's way, clinging to my (his) opinion: "Accident!"—that is, Beowulf's victory has no moral meaning; all life is chance. But the fear that
it may not all be accident strikes back instantly, prodded a little by
childhood notions of the cross—blood guilt, one's desperate need to
be a good boy, be loved both by one's parents and by that terrifying
superfather whose otherness cannot be more frighteningly expressed
than by the fact that he lives beyond the stars. So for all his conscious
belief that it's all accident, Grendel *chooses* death, morally aligning himself with God (hence trying to save himself); that is, against his will he
notices that he seems to "desire the fall." Abruptly the nightmare landscape shifts, from looking "down" past the tree into the abyss of night
to another source of vertigo, looking down from the edge of a cliff. I
did not consciously make this shift because of the nightmare I'd had
in my sleep the night before I wrote this page; rather, I noticed as I
made the shift that in fact what I was writing was a nightmare that I'd
had and until that instant had forgotten.

A day or two before, my family and I had been watching Olympic
ski jumpers practice—a terrifying business, to me at least, frightened
as I am by heights. In a dream, the night before the writing of this
passage, I'd found myself moving very slowly—but inexorably—
toward the edge of the ski jump, the snow below me unspeakably far
away. I'd felt in my nightmare, for whatever reason, exactly this same
sense that I was willing the fall, in spite of myself. (I think there is
some strange pun in the word "fall"; at any rate, it's a word I've often

used elsewhere in its Edenic sense: so that the fear I felt as I was
writing this passage—or enduring the entrancement—may have to do
with moral paradox of the kind the unconscious takes wicked delight
in: willing his death, Grendel is unconsciously trying to please God so
that God will not slaughter him; willing "the Fall," he is defying the
God he hates and fears.) Grendel feels the movement in himself to be
in some way the movement of the universe. He is like "an ocean current," such a current as brought Beowulf to kill him; he feels that something inside him (his heart, his *id*) is at one with that current; and since
earlier in the novel it was Grendel himself who lived "inside" (a cave),
he is, since he houses the *id* monster, the mountain whose steeps he
fears; he is some fabled mystery ("deep sea wonder"); and if the whole
night sky is conceived as God's cave, then Grendel, "dread night monarch astir in his cave," is God. At the time I wrote the passage, I made
all these connections (ocean current, monster, sea wonder, etc.) without consciously thinking: the mystical oneness, the calmly accepted
paradox, were inherent in the entrancement.

The only point I mean to make out of this long and possibly self-
indulgent analysis is this: All I myself know for sure, when I come out
of one of these trance moments, is that I seem to have been taken over
by some muse. Insofar as I'm able to remember what happened, it
seems to me that it was this: for a moment the real process of our
dreams has been harnessed. The magic key goes in, all the tumblers
fall at once and the door swings open. Or: mental processes that are
usually discrete for some reason act together. I was of course conscious,
throughout my writing of *Grendel*, that what I was trying to talk about
(or dramatize, or seek to get clear) was an annoying, sometimes painful
disharmony in my own mental experience, a conflict between a wish
for certainty, a sort of timid and legalistic rationality, on the one hand,
and, on the other, an inclination toward childish optimism, what I
might now describe as an occasional, flickering affirmation of all that
was best in my early experience of Christianity. Surrounded by university people who had, as we say, "outgrown religion," and feeling
uneasy about joining their party because to do so might be a cowardly
surrender and a betrayal of my background, though refusing to do so
might also be cowardice, and a betrayal of myself, I had gloomed
through writers like Jean-Paul Sartre who seemed confident that they
knew what they were talking about (I was not convinced); I'd joined
churches and, finding them distasteful, had left; and I'd become, more
or less by accident, a specialist in medieval Christian poetry, including

of course *Beowulf*, source of, among other things, the quasi-mystical macrocosm/microcosm equations at the end of the passage I've been discussing. All the elements to be fused in the trance moment were in place, like the assembled components of the Frankenstein monster's body before the lightning strikes. What I really can't explain is the lightning. It may have to do with entering as fully as possible into the imaginary experience of the character, getting "outside" oneself (a paradox, since the character to be entered is a projection of the writer's self). It may have to do with the sense of mental strain one experiences at such moments: the whole mind seems tightened like a muscle, fierce with concentration. Anyway, if one is lucky the lightning strikes, and the madness at the core of the fictional idea for a moment glows on the page.

From "An Interview with John Gardner"

[Geraldine DeLuca]:   We're doing this issue on writers who write both for children and adults, and I guess a good place to start is by asking why you write for children.

[John Gardner]:   It started accidentally, the way all writing starts. When my kids were growing up, each year I would give them a Christmas present of a story. I'd always make up the stories. Then one day you make an especially polished one and you get to thinking about how a children's story ought to work to be really classic and especially interesting to kids. You want kids to love the story and to buy the book for their children their grandchildren and their great great great grandchildren and so on. So, while I was making up those Christmas stories I got to thinking about it. And as I was doing children's stories and enjoying them I got to thinking about all the things that Bettelheim talks about—about the way you really can say things that are very important to kids in these stories. For instance, the book I got my daughter to grow up on was *1001 Nights*. It seems to me that's a wonderful book on how to be a girl—because you have to be cunning, you have to be graceful, but not weak. That's an amazing book. I feel that that book *is* about how to grow up a woman in a chauvinist society and not lose everything. And I think that the book to buy a boy is Malory's *Morte D'Arthur* so that he'll know he's supposed to be a knight. . . . So it's pretty moralistic I guess. But I think fiction is pretty moral; I think all art is pretty moral.

GD: Do you feel more moralistic when you're writing for children than for adults?

JG: No. And I don't think good fiction of any kind, for adults or children, tells lies. If you tell the absolute truth, it will be difficult and complex. . . . Any place where you lie, you lose your credibility and

Excerpted from "An Interview with John Gardner" by Roni Natov and Geraldine DeLuca, *The Lion and the Unicorn* 2, no. 1 (Spring 1978): 114–20, 129–30, 132–34. © 1978 *The Lion and the Unicorn*. Reprinted by permission of the Johns Hopkins University Press.

the book becomes worthless. In any children's story, the kid has to know that he's in good hands. It's true for adults too: as soon as you begin to suspect a story, you begin to get a little bored. One of the awful things in adult fiction is the unreliable narrator. I know that it's amusing for the writer and I know that it's an interesting kind of game to play when you're an English professor. But it's basically unsatisfying. It's one thing to do what Donald Barthelme does. Donald Barthelme is very good. He doesn't really have unreliable narrators. His narrators are people who don't know the answers. They're just lost. But the flat out smart aleck unreliable narrator is just a nuisance. . . .

. . . [T]here's a change taking place in children's books that's curious to me. For example, *The Nightmares of Geranium Street* is a wonderful book but it makes me nervous. It takes an honest look at the ghetto, but it seems to me important that a book give you hope and give you models, how to act and how to think, and that book is very uninspiring. There isn't any sunlight. The only sunlight is the compassion you feel, and at the end one of the main characters, who's a junkie, gets carted off to jail. She had no choice anyway, she is a nice lady, that's the way life was for her, but her daughter is left. You don't know what's going to happen to her and the Nightmares, the gang, are left in the same ghetto and that's the way the world is. It *is* a good book. It just makes me nervous, that's all. If I'm going to write for those kids, I'd rather deal with them in a fantasy world where everything's not bleak or where there's a hint of sunlight in the background. On the other hand, I don't like authors like C. S. Lewis, although my kids loved him. He's a melodramatist. He's got good guys and bad guys. He's a class man. The upper class is good; the lower class is bad. In a C. S. Lewis novel, the kid who's from the lower class is always untrustworthy—devious, sneaky, cockney. I hate that. I think that kids know that that's not so good, yet the story's interesting, so they go on. But if they go on, it undermines something. They don't trust Lewis but then they begin to think, well maybe he's right. And then you just don't have any fun in the story. The fairy tales are different. In the fairy tales, bad is bad but good is also bad. You know, for example, that the good little girl in the fairy tale who knows that the stepmother is going to chop off her head when she goes to sleep will get behind the bad sister and move the bad sister into her place so that the bad sister gets it. That's bad, but it's cunning and necessary.

[Roni Natov]: We found that the characters in your books are ordinary; you explore the complexity of ordinary people. You give them so much space and intensity. It's an unusual picture of middle America. In *Nickel Mountain*, for example, there is so much detail—about the restaurant, Callie, etc. Or about the police officer and his work in *The Sunlight Dialogues*.

JG: That's a curious quality when it comes to writing for children, because one of the things I find interesting is applying modern novelistic standards to the original fairy tales. For example, in the traditional fairy tale, Cinderella sweeps ashes but you don't get any description of how to sweep ashes. Whereas in my story "The King of the Hummingbirds" where the kid spends the night working—you know, cleaning pots and pans—I describe it. The focus is different. In traditional fairy tales, the focus is on knights, princes, princesses. But when I write, I use middle class characters; that is, even if they're kings, I make them think in middle class ways. Then I have to deal with the differences between the middle and upper class. The aristocracy always thinks it's right, and if it doesn't think it's right, it's not going to tell you. For example, in Nietzsche there are two moralities: the slave morality of the Jewish man and the true morality of the Prussian officer who's in a position of power. I don't like a single thing Nietzsche ever said. I don't like his politics. I think he's a Nazi. I like the middle class morality. In "The King of the Hummingbirds," the king doesn't know how to solve the problem, the knight doesn't know, nobody knows. But the king and the knight, in their middle class way, bungle it up together. In traditional fairy tales, the third son wins because he is in fact a natural aristocrat, he's your true prince in disguise. But solutions in my stories do not come about because of the wonderful power of a true-born aristocrat.

GD: Why do you choose fairy tales for your children's work—what do find in the genre?

JG: I like the simplicity. In realistic fiction you spend a lot of time documenting things. That's okay if you want to describe what it's like to live in a certain town, but I want to get at the moral side of each tale, and every tale presents some basic idea of how to live with other people. The fundamental issue is that you live in a world in which you're not really sure of what's going on. For example, you're walking down Broadway and you see two guys fighting, a little guy and a big guy, and your impulse is to break up the fight. But it may be that the little guy just slept with the big guy's wife and you don't know that, so any action you might take is likely to be absurd. But you may have to act anyway, and sometimes you make a mistake and you may have to pay for it. It isn't fair. That's why I think cunning is a very fine virtue. That's why I like Odysseus and the other heroes who used it.

GD: Could you explain something about your fairy tale "The Griffin and the Wise [Old] Philosopher"? How does the wise philosopher know the griffin's going to leave town at the end?

JG: He doesn't. That's a fairy tale that's basically a joke. It's for older kids, which is true of most of my fairy tales. All of them, in fact, with the possible exception of "Dragon, Dragon," I really meant for kids who have been through fairy tales and are ready for slight variety. A kid at that age has probably heard of the Heisenberg principle because that's one of the favorite principles of modern mathematics. The Heisenberg principle is the uncertainty principle and the fairy tale takes place in the town of Heizenburg where the griffin, by his nature, sets up uncertainty. So all the philosopher does is just follow the uncertainty principle to its end and as it happens in this case it works out.

RN: We get a sense in the children's stories—although it's quite clear in your adult novels too—that there's a figure who represents chaos who enters the world and sets up a threatening situation. That, in turn, encourages someone to figure out how order is going to be restored. Do you see that as a preoccupation in your work?

JG: Yes. Basically my view of reality is that it's a little chaotic—not completely, but chaotic enough so that you don't know what's going to happen to you. Life is full of improbability and we all have ways of dealing with it. Nice clear codes. I mean, don't slam the screen door and everything will be all right. The problem in my stories usually is that a character has his own nice neat code but he has to abandon it. Then, by abandoning it and sort of rolling with the punches, he's successful. In "Dragon, Dragon," for instance, the two older brothers know what's right. One of them knows that to kill a dragon you have to use intellect; the other knows you have to use strength. But they both fail. The younger brother simply takes his father's advice, which is absurd, and he succeeds. And Gudgekin the Thistle Girl knows what we all know, that you're not supposed to pity yourself, you're not supposed to go around crying, lamenting your lot. You're supposed to care about other people. That's true, but once in a while you do feel sorry for yourself. What happens is she finally gives up the code and she becomes a nihilist. Then she doesn't believe anybody; she thinks that she's the most miserable person in the world. Ultimately she finds a kind of middle ground. I think that that is standard in my fiction. I do it in different ways. . . .

GD: What kind of response have you gotten to your children's books? From children or from reviewers?

JG: Kind of respectful. There's a problem for writers who are in my position. You don't really get honest criticism. Once in a while someone will say what he really thinks, but mostly they don't. With the last *New York Times* reviews of *In the Suicide Mountains* or the *Child's Bestiary*, for example, it was perfectly clear that the writers of both reviews didn't like the books at all, but they wouldn't say it. I would rather hear that they didn't like them. It's a curious thing. Judged by the standards of entertainment, the adventures in *In the Suicide Mountains* aren't very interesting. The *Oz* books are more interesting. But judged by a different standard, that is to say, that *In the Suicide Mountains* is talking about suicide, then it's a worthwhile thing. But since you've got to start with the premise that this is an entertainment, another wacky Gardner children's book, it wasn't very readable. I think that was the problem, but the reviewer didn't say enough about it. I think that if it is true that it's a boring book for kids, then that's a problem.

GD: Have you had any response from kids?

JG: Yes, I've had a lot of response from kids, but the problem is that all the kids are doctors' and lawyers' children and they really like my stuff. And they know me too. The main thing I discovered is that if you read these stories to children too early, they get bored. If you read "Dragon, Dragon" to a five year old, the kid will go around remembering that verse *Dragon, dragon, how do you do? I've come from the king to murder you*, but the story has too many dead spots for him.

GD: Right, they're ironic.

RN: It's a funny book, very funny. I liked the fact that the king is exposed for being very self-involved and at the end the queen is glaring at him. His flaw is not corrected. He just remains human and flawed. The *Gudgekin* stories didn't move me as much.

JG: Oh, I liked *Gudgekin*.

GD: I did too. One night when I was very depressed, I wrote a poem based on it about withholding from yourself the way she did. . . .

GD: What children's books did you read as a child?

JG: I don't remember. I read a lot of children's books. I never liked Lewis Carroll as a child. I guess you have to be a girl. And it's a sort of mathematical world. I thought I should like it. But I didn't. I like sentimental slop like *Winnie-the-Pooh*. I loved *Winnie-the-Pooh*.

GD: It's very vintage sentimentality. It is precious but he does it so well. He's so damn witty at being sentimental.

JG: That's true. The characters were real characters. A character like Eeyore is amazing.

RN: And Eeyore is not sentimental.

JG: He's a lot less sentimental. In fact he's got some really good lines.

RN: Do you read children's books now? Did you read them to your kids?

JG: I read a lot of children's books. Sometimes friends write them. Sometimes they're sent to me because somebody liked them. But I don't read anything unless I have to. There are so many books I have to read because people sent them to me for comment. Once in a while if you're really lucky, you get someone like John Fowles but most of them are pretty bad. . . .

RN: Getting back to children's books, I noticed that in *Dragon, Dragon* you seem to be dealing with what's traditionally thought of as evil—the dragon figure and the giant figure and so on—as if they are funny, amusing. You seem to be saying that instead of being evil, they're messy, chaotic. For example, the dragon is killed because he's laughing and totally out of control. Did you have a preconception, that you wanted to convey, that evil is not really dangerous? Did you want to transform things that are generally frightening to children, to make them less frightening?

JG: No, not really. The thing about the oldest brother and the second brother is that they have their dignity. They know how to do things. The youngest brother has no dignity. He just does what his father says; it's silly but he does it. He's wearing this heavy armor and carrying this ridiculous sword and he obviously can't do anything. But he recites the verse and the dragon laughs at him, especially when he says that ridiculous poem. I don't know, it's some complicated thing about dignity. About how on one hand one ought not to have any dignity. It's a silly thing to be carrying around. On the other hand, when somebody really insults you, that's the time to get mad. When the dragon laughs at the youngest brother, that's when he attacks. Which is a reasonable response.

From "Letter to Burton [Weber]"

Dear Burton,

On account of your question on A. Gordon Pym (why is the ending scary), I've reread Poe, everything I have in my 5 vol. edition. (I know the question wasn't all that serious, but since I like Poe, as I guess you don't, and since I couldn't answer the question off hand, I figured I better reread.) I had a magnificent time. When I finished I knew everything, and I was ready to write an article praising Poe and showing what he does, but then I found out Richard Wilbur already noticed and told the world. Which is terrific because it freed me to do a more interesting thing, which is write a story (novel) which is a marriage of Poe and Melville, that is, a story in the manner of Melville, following a plot by Poe (A. Gordon Pym, or Ms found in a bottle), the trip of a maniacal Ahab to the south pole. It treats Poe's political theories and plays them against Melville's (Poe a Southern aristocrat, pro-slavery man, the best possible version of a Tate type Southern agrarian, and Melville, in his own phrase, a "cosmic democrat."), Poe's and Melville's aesthetic theories (Poe, like Eliot, concerned about emotional tightness): a story should be, Poe's practice proves, allegorical; but its first appeal is unified emotion, so that Poe is finally exactly like Coleridge, believing that stories and poems are about metaphysics, ethics, aesthetics, psychology, and so on, but sets "Truth" lower than "Beauty," or emotional integrity. Melville, on the other hand, judging both by his practice and his letters, makes "Truth" paramount, clearly and repeatedly violating "unity of effect"—the chief criticism fools level against *Moby Dick*—yet justifies his truths (or validates, or beautifies) by the finest prose rhythms ever created by an English speaker. Poe's sentences labor (successfully, in my opinion) for emotional effect but are indifferent to rhythm. Melville actually puts himself in the way of effect—see, for instance, the Town-Ho narrative in *Moby Dick* where

Excerpted from a photocopy of an undated letter in the John Gardner Papers collection at the University of Rochester Library (box 15). © by Georges Borchardt, Inc. Printed by permission of the Estate of John Gardner and Georges Borchardt, Inc.

he perversely, and consciously (as his own words show), interrupts his narrative with questions by the Spaniards to whom it's being told. What Melville felt, of course, was that gripping stories are too fucking easy: the reader must be reminded again and again that he's to take this stuff *seriously*. I sympathize with him, though of course I don't agree. I gave my "Ravages of Spring" to Helen Vergette, a superb reader, and she missed everything I was doing because it sounded so good. What the greatest artists have understood—Homer, Vergil, Shakespeare, Chaucer—is that a superbly told story *will* be understood on its finest levels sooner or later. One need not make fun of one's less intense readers or put them off. God loves them too. (The greatest writers are also the greatest lovers of mankind, even when they condemn.), and, finally, Poe's and Melville's metaphysical systems. It came to me (though no one will believe me, so I won't trouble to point it out to the general) that the Lee Shore chapter in *Moby Dick* is about Edgar Poe, alias Bulkington, the sailor who dies at sea, that is, comes to his apotheosis. My story (novel) is called "Augusta," imitating Poe's trick of using symbolic woman-names as story names. She is the Southern idea of democracy, doomed from the start, though supremely beautiful, because of the institution of slavery, without which she cannot exist. Poe's politics lead to revolution or civil war, Melville's to atheism. Both monumental sorrows, however, drive you back to Melville's and Poe's Christianity—or, more exactly, religion. (An atheist can make it until his son dies.) So, in short, what makes the ending of A. Gordon Pym so terrifying is that it's [a] careful symbolic treatment of cosmic dissolution. The novel, remember, was written by a very young man. The "boring" early parts present, among other things, the first literary cannibalism game, the first convincing burial alive, the first cliff-hanger gimmick (done a la Sartre: the narrator thinks he will fall, then desires the fall, then realizes his *freedom* to fall, then falls *to prove his freedom* and then is saved, as in all those movies of the thirties). If you enable yourself to come on it cold and innocent, it's fantastic! The best commentary on Pym, as Wilbur has shown (and as I discovered without his help) is Poe's magnificent *Eureka: A Prose Poem*. There, a hundred years ahead of his time, Poe discovered that "Space and Duration are *identical*," invented the Hubbelean theory of the universe (adumbrated in the *Vedas*), discovered what Schopenhauer discovered about the one will and individuated wills (restated, wrongly, by Bergson), and discovered, before the invention of existentialism, the answer to existentialism (that it's sick—i.e., a philosophy made up by a paranoid). Consider, for example, this: "On the Universal agglomeration and dissolution, we can readily conceive that a new and perhaps totally different series of conditions may ensue—another creation and irradiation, returning into itself—another action and reaction of the Divine Will. Guiding our imaginations by that omniprevalent law of laws, the law of periodicity, are we not, indeed, more then justified in entertaining a belief—let us say, rather, in indulging a hope—that the processes we have here ventured to contemplate will be renewed forever, and forever, and forever; a novel Universe swelling into existence, and then subsiding into nothingness, at every throb of the Heart Divine?

"And now—this Heart Divine—what is it? *It is our own.*" (Poe's italics.) Poe discovers, in *Eureka*[,] that matter is thought (Whitehead), that the universe is expanding at an accelerating rate—a rate terrifying to consider (he liked that part!) (Einstein), and suggested that the process must reverse itself into universal collapse (Hubble, part I), to be followed by a new explosion (Hubble, part II). All this without benefit of the red or blue shifts. He argues that without time there can be no space, and that for this to be true there must be possible a transformation from matter to "the electrical principle," or, he says, *energia*, Aristotle's word for Plot, Poe's for God. In A. Gordon Pym, both the boring parts and the thrilling, Poe dramatizes this metaphysical vision. When the Antarctic current catches the narrator and his friend (representing mind and body) and the black savage (representing the perverse body, irascibility and concupiscence at their worst—Poe hated blacks), the meaning is that one is caught in the accelerating current of dissolution, heading toward total disaster and apotheosis (the huge, snow white man—Christ, of course). The closer they get to the Antarctic, the stranger things become. Throughout the novel, the narrator has been succeeding by reason; but little by little, reason has become less and less useful. On the island of Too-witt (to wit:) reason gives clear but wrong answers, as Poe's note after the "unfinished" ending shows (the note is a masterpiece of ironic misinformation worthy of Melville at his most ferocious). But in the final plunge, the rush toward the heart of things, reason becomes totally meaningless: in fact consciousness itself becomes meaningless. Gigantic, strange birds cry "*Tekeli-li!*" Scholarly attempts to explain this word are comically wrongheaded. The whole point is, there is *no* way man can understand what is going on. He's in a foreign element, the realm of beautiful and terrifying spirit, the kingdom of death and resurrection. Eagerly, joyfully, body and mind hurtle toward dissolution, and despite all the eagerness and joy, they are scared to death. The heart attack of the universe—*It is our own.* Poe's clumsy first novel is, in my opinion, a magnificent proof that Melville was right. Unity of effect is trash beside metaphysical truth. It is also true, of course, that Poe's best writing—Casque of Amontillado, House of Usher, Ulalume, The Raven, and—above all—Ligeia) are poems of unified effect. (I meant, by the way, "poems.") Read in a studied Virginia accent, they are unbeatable works of art, in my stubborn judgment. But this happens, I think, because Poe was confident of his theory, and even though it was wrong, it gave him confidence—a matter more important than one can say: If you *know* you are right, even if you're wrong, you're convincing.

I sound, I admit, like a shit-ass American literature teacher (I hate American literature teachers) trying desperately to defend his subject. But remember I am *not* an American literature teacher. My chief loyalties are to Homer, Vergil, Chaucer, Shakespeare (whom I do not like), and Eliot, alias Wallace Stevens. Nevertheless, I love only philosophical poets, and I am a modern man whose philosophical problems are modern ones. What finally matters

I forgot to mention the greatest of them all, Blake!

is not that Poe had a thousand thousand faults, but that he *said* something—something profoundly important, profoundly American; that he said, as a committed Southerner, something deeply moving to at least two true Yankees, Melville and Me, and that in an age of nonsense, he produced art.

Now I will lecture you on Mahler. . . .

. . . Lest I seem an enthusiast, I grant that Mahler is not as good as Vergil or Homer, just as Poe is a joke beside Chaucer. But that means nothing, finally. The best one normally hopes for in life is, say, Edward Taylor or Charles Brock[den] Brown. I am better, thank God, than them. (This picks up the theme introduced earlier, I am like Mahler.)

I have just reread the above (from the top). Boringest fucking letter I ever read. Ah well, be well.

Yr hmbl svt,
John

"Outline for 'The Warden'"

One wishes to be whole (the ultimate *unorganized* (A) life)—entranced (the mystical state). One is *imprisoned in logic* (B), body.—time & space.

Courses of action.		
Malist Crime 1: *intellectual* or *rational*	1)	Refuse to admit condition A, and hate B as inadequate, inescapable. The pain of B *teaches* us to long, futilely, for A. [Josef Malist.] All such longing is misdirected, mere illusion. For self-expression, fiercely attack illusions—the good state, art, religion, science.
Narrator	2)	Take no stand on A; act pragmatically to relieve the pain of B, knowing you must fail in advance. [Mild (venial) guilt is uncertainty about A.]
Heller	3)	Affirm A, though it seems absurd, & do as in 2. [The Jewish answer.] [Guilt as in 2.]
Crime 2 *concupiscent* The Children (other prisoners)	4)	Take no stand on A, & do not act for (cf. 2) others. Pursue "pleasure."
Crime 3 *Old Man* *irascible*	5)	Affirm A, enjoy suffering as prerequisite. [Old man]

rational (hate of B)		
irascible *The Warden*	6)	Affirm A, hate or feel indifferent to B; waste your life awaiting experience of A until you doubt & hate it. [Guilt—*mortal*—the Warden].
concupisc.		
The Father	7)	Affirm A and B, moving between them (the artist).
The Wife	8)	Misunderstand both A & B, yet live within both—less efficiently. (As a faulty parent, comforter, friend.)

Render: the trance state(s), difficulty of achieving them or even recognizing them.

Father (gardener, painter, musician) talks of Malist's coming execution. (Malist has been dead for months.)

The children eat, play, refuse to help their mother, refuse to read the Bible (which the narrator does not entirely believe—his father does.) Remind the narrator of pleasure-seeking prisoners.

The mother, in a daze (trance), lets them be. She is religious, herself—prays, etc.—but fails to see that it matters for the children.

Father on ghosts. He's not sure he's ever seen one, but he knows, from art, about the infinite (A), and individuated Will (Schopenhauer).

Father says Malist's death will be a great blow to the Warden, & exactly describes the situation.

Narrator suspects Father knows M is dead, & is cheating, not intuiting. [Time confusion in the infinite mind.]

Father (as if irrelevantly) on art (vision vs. intellectual manipulation)—in response to narrator's story of old man. Plays violin.

Narr's wife equates children & father. Father says, rightly, not the same at all.

Death of old man. Heller, after asking abt. Narr & Warden conversation, takes Narr to see corpse. Tells Narr of old man's pleasure in pain. They go up to Warden to ask permission to bury old man in churchyard because he's been, they think, deprived of his civil rights. Narr hears pacing, Heller does not. Then neither is quite sure. They bury old man. The churchyard creek (symbol of the infinite). Narr's sense that Warden is nearby, observing him. Gets a glimpse, dismisses it. (Heller on *Khiseth?*) The Jewish ambiguity. They talk, sitting on

gravestones, of Malist, whom Heller understands. (Birds, trees, etc.)
H. tells of Malist's attempted escape, his own strangely automatic reaction. Understands, also, why the Warden hated him (M).

(Cut) Narr with father, family. Learns that father has often seen Warden near church. So has wife. Sends for Heller. They open W's door
and find him in creek near church (suicide), badly decomposed.

"Commentary on 'The King's Indian'"

Joshua Flint (con-man) & his daughter Miranda take over the whaler *Jerusalem*, making Captain Dirge their victim (through hypnotism) because they believe the hoax story of the *Jerusalem* seen sinking again and again throughout history, just off the Vanishing Isles. They've fooled others often with their time-travel trick; but they've come to hope & half-believe it's possible, for all their cynicism. As on the stage, they're unscrupulous—

The sly American con-man (Davy Crockett, Brer Rabbit, Coyote, Jesse James, etc.) Josh E. Frye, Pres. Nixon.

(Wilkins is the book's "cannie half breed, Sam Smiley") (Book has picture of Flint grown old— also Miranda at 25 or so.)

even using slaves. Once at sea, they murder Dirge & substitute an automaton. (Flint takes disguise of a blind prophet.) Jonathan Upchurch & Wilkins, also con-men, survive. It's because Jonathan might know Flint that he & his daughter become interested in him. (Flint, Jonathan learns from his book, was a midwesterner, as Jon. claims to be.) It's Wilkins who made the automaton, also started the hoax which fooled the Flints. (The dog, Jester, is really "Swami Alastor, Wonderdog.") Wilkins also made the trick trap to the hold, etc.

The mysterious portrait is really an hypnotic device, operating on Augusta.

In the encounter with the pirate ship, the Yugoslavs recognize Jeremiah (i.e., Flint), and the dying one says: "Escape! Save yourselves! The Captain—Flint!" Seems to mean that Flint is Captain aboard the pirate ship—really means, stay with the pirates, escape the ship where

Flint, i.e., Jeremiah, is—and also save the Captain. (Jonathan &
Augusta sneak aboard privateer as common seamen. They move
among the crew; Yugoslavs come up to them, having seen Jeremiah. A
"thrown" knife kills him—but really, *Augusta* kills him.)

Mariner—story teller
Angel—angel
Guest—listener

Part 3

THE CRITICS

Introduction

The following excerpts from other critics' commentaries represent the best work that has been done to date on Gardner's short fiction. The first passage is from Howell's essay "The Wound and the Albatross: John Gardner's Apprenticeship." It provides a factual account of the childhood accident in which Gardner's brother Gilbert died (a pivotal event in Gardner's life and career), as well as Howell's assessment of Gardner's treatment of the accident in the story "Redemption." The next group of selections, from Cowart's chapter "From Angst to Affirmation: *The King's Indian*," includes a passage from his introductory remarks, a substantial portion of his analysis of the title novella, and a part of his conclusion. The third excerpt, from Deluca and Natov's essay "Modern Moralities for Children: John Gardner's Children's Books," is from perhaps the only critical essay published to date that deals exclusively with Gardner's books for children. The fourth returns to Cowart's *Arches and Light* for a portion of his chapter "Theme and Variations," which deals with *The Art of Living and Other Stories*. The passage reprinted includes Cowart's analysis of "Vlemk the Box-Painter." The final selection is from Morris's chapter on *The Art of Living and Other Stories* and includes his discussion of "The Library Horror."

John M. Howell

Like Coleridge's Ancient Mariner, John Gardner told his tale again and again. On April 4, 1945, three months away from his twelfth birthday, he accidentally killed his younger brother Gilbert. The trauma of this moment haunted him for most of his life. It created a psychic wound that had much to do with his becoming a writer. . . .

Gardner relived his brother Gilbert's death in agonizing nightmares and flashbacks. Though he distorted the facts of the accident in both telling and writing about it, interviews with his mother Priscilla and his sister Sandy help to put most of the facts back in their place.

In a recent interview, Priscilla Gardner described the day of Gilbert's death as a "beautiful, beautiful spring day, balmy, lovely. And Bud [John Gardner's family nickname] was going to the other [farm] with a tractor and a low, big flat wagon." He was eleven, his sister was four, and Gilbert (nicknamed "Gib") was six. When Sandy and Gib asked if they might go with Bud, Priscilla, seeing the wagon, said yes, never thinking to ask how they were coming back.

As Bud drove the big Farmall F-20 tractor back down the road toward his home, he was pulling, instead of the wagon, a two-ton roller called a cultipacker. Sandy was sitting in his lap, steering, and Gib was sitting on the cross-bar which attached the cultipacker to the tractor. As they came down a low hill, the tractor ran out of gas and stumbled to a halt, throwing Gib to the road. Sandy Gardner Smith says that when she turned, she saw the cultipacker crushing Gib's skull. Then Bud turned, saw, and, according to him, froze. Though he would later say that he could have jammed on the brakes and saved Gib, his sister insists, as does her mother, that it was too late to make a difference.

A neighbor coming down the road stopped and brought Bud, Sandy, and Gib's body back to the Gardners' home. Sandy Smith remembers

Excerpted from "The Wound and the Albatross: John Gardner's Apprenticeship" by John M. Howell, in *Thor's Hammer: Essays on John Gardner,* ed. Jeff Henderson (Conway: University of Central Arkansas Press, 1985), 1–16. © 1985 by John M. Howell. Reprinted by permission of the author.

being so much in shock after the accident that she was obsessed with the notion that her mother would be angry because her dress was spattered with blood. Bud was convinced, however, that his brother was dead and that he was responsible, and, according to his mother, immediately told her, "I've killed Gilbert." She remembers telling him, "Oh, Bud, of course you haven't." But he insisted: "Mom, I have." He believed, she said, that he could have stopped the tractor, but, she continued, "he couldn't have stopped it. You can't stop a big roller coming down a hill. And I said, 'Nobody could stop that. No human power could do it, and God doesn't work that way.'" But Gardner was unable to reconcile the ways of God, man, and machine. Had there been a choice? Did the empty gas tank, the stumbling motor, the incline of the hill, and the inertia of the cultipacker—all leave Gilbert's death to chance? At one moment Gardner accepted the consolation that Gilbert's death was the result of chance—pure accident. At the next moment he insisted that Gilbert's death was, as he told his mother the day of Gilbert's death, his fault—that he had, through a failure of will, allowed Gilbert to die. In short, Gardner's consciousness became a battleground for the classic duel between determinism and free will, and he would spend the rest of his life trying to reconcile these competing forces.

Gardner explored the accident and its metaphysical implications from the beginning of his career to its violent end, using many different masks and parallel actions. But finally, during the spring of 1975—and possibly later—he wrote about it directly in the novel "Stillness," now slated for publication by Knopf with the unfinished novel "Shadows."

"Stillness" is openly autobiographical—so subjective, in fact, that Gardner does not quite find his thematic focus, one of the reasons, perhaps, that he put the novel away. He gives the autobiographical protagonist the name "Martin Orrick"—and the nickname "Buddy." Buddy's wife is called "Joan," the name of Gardner's first wife; while Buddy's sister is named "Sandy" and his brother is named "Gilbert." The thematic question of determinism vs. free will is directly stated rather than dramatized as in the story "Redemption," written a year or so later. Indeed, the following passage from "Stillness" functions as a kind of expository gloss on the more concentrated and poetically realized story about the same experience:

> Causes and effects are not neatly separable, as we sometimes find
> them in fiction. Martin Orrick's nature helped the accident to hap-

pen, and the accident helped to shape his nature, each feeding on the other as past and present do, or ends and means, or—as Orrick would say—the brain's two lobes. In any event, part of what Joan's mother called his "darkness" had to do with this: One day, in a farm accident, Martin—that is, Buddy—ran over and killed his brother Gilbert. It was an ugly and stupid accident which, even at the last moment, Buddy could have prevented by hitting the tractor brakes; but he was unable to think, or rather thought unclearly, and so watched it happen, as he would watch it happen in his mind, with undiminished clarity, again and again until the day he died. (68)

The narrative then relates how Buddy found at least partial psychic health through playing the French horn. And it makes clear that Buddy "would never be a really first-rate player," but that he was superior to those close to his own age and thus he began to "think himself much better than he was . . ." (85). However many times Gardner portrayed the ambiguous causes and devastating effects of his brother's death, he never did so with such candor and intensity as in "Redemption," published in *Atlantic Monthly* (May 1977) and reprinted in *The Art of Living and Other Stories* (1981). Like "Stillness," the narrative of "Redemption" moves from the accident to the guilt to the French horn. But it does so, as suggested, with a concentration of image and theme that the earlier narrative lacks. And there is, at the same time, a greater manipulation of the facts for their emotional and thematic effects.

We know, from Priscilla Gardner's account, that the accident took place on a road. In "Redemption," however, Gardner places the accident on a level field, where Jack Hawthorne is steering the tractor, his little sister Phoebe is sitting on its fender, and his little brother David is riding on the cultipacker. By the same token, the facts of David's fatal injury have also been recast: "The scream came not from David, who never got a sound out, but from their five-year-old sister. . . . When Jack turned to look, the huge iron wheels had reached his brother's pelvis. He kept driving, and imagining, in the same stab of thought, that perhaps his brother would survive. Blood poured from David's mouth" (30). This manipulation of the facts is obviously intended to objectify an emotion that would not have been inspired by the mechanical failure of a tractor on a hill, despite its tragic consequences. But Gardner was not supposed to let his siblings ride on the farm machinery; of this he was guilty. But in writing about the experience Gardner magnifies the responsibility, and thus the guilt of his fictional projection, by giving him a choice that he does not make.

Sandy Smith indicates that when she looked back she saw the cultipacker crushing her little brother's head. Priscilla Gardner maintains, by the same token, that the cultipacker did not, as "Redemption" indicates, crush her son's legs. Indeed, Gardner may himself contradict his fictional representation when he makes the seemingly factual statements that David "never got a sound out" and that "Blood poured from [his] mouth." Both statements suggest that David (like Gilbert) died from an injury to his chest and/or skull. However, by placing gas in the tractor's tank and the tractor on a level field, and by having the cultipacker travel up David's body from his legs to his head, Gardner widened the space of the action—thus the time of Jack's spiritual paralysis and the agony of guilt and memory.

Metaphorically speaking, Gardner's distortion of the facts objectified the spirit of the various kinds of consolations he was offered at the time of Gilbert's death. Apart from the primary consolation that the accident was not his fault, that no one could have stopped the cultipacker in a situation like that, there was the secondary consolation that it was a blessing that Gilbert had not survived, hopelessly brain damaged and crippled. That is, on the one hand, Gardner was merely part of the machinery of Gilbert's death; on the other hand, he was, effectively, a mercy killer, "reacting as he would to a half-crushed farm animal." But for Gardner, meaning demanded a choice. There is no redemption if there is no guilt. There is no guilt if there is no choice.

"Redemption" follows [the novel] "Stillness" in portraying how the protagonist (Jack Hawthorne) turns to the French horn for the therapy of an emotional focus and release. Again, however, there is a significant thematic difference between the two versions, a difference resulting from Gardner's dramatic presentation of Jack Hawthorne's illusions and self-discoveries. Significantly, Gardner had, between writing the novel "Stillness" (in progress, spring 1975) and the story "Redemption" (in progress, fall 1976), started writing the key chapters of *On Moral Fiction*. It was perhaps inevitable, therefore, that he would underline this thesis on the morality of art in the most autobiographical of his fictions. In "Stillness," Buddy Orrick is filled with feelings of guilt and self-pity. In "Redemption," however, Jack Hawthorne is filled with rage as well as guilt, and he focuses this rage on his father, who seems to get most of the community's sympathy when, convulsed with grief, he disappears on his motorcycle for nearly three weeks, and then returns, the prodigal father, to be forgiven by his wife, daughter, and relatives in a way that embitters Jack. In his father's absence Jack had longed for the same kind of isolation from the tragedy as well as the community: "If what he felt was hatred, it was terrible, desperate envy, too; his father all alone, uncompromised, violent, cut off as if by centuries from the warmth, chatter, and smells of the kitchen, the dimness of stained glass where he, Jack, sat every Sunday between his mother and sister, looking toward the pulpit where in the old days his father had sometimes read the lesson, soft-voiced but aloof from the timid-eyed flock, Christ's sheep" (41). Feeling rejected, Jack rejects, in turn, "Christ's sheep." And he is especially bitter when his father gains a new dignity as well as oneness with the community after his penitent return. When his father speaks now in church he is no longer aloof, but speaks as if "some mere suffering sheep among sheep" (43). He has, in the terms of the narrative, been spiritually redeemed.

Jack will have none of it. After raging against himself, berating himself for a failure to love, and contemplating suicide, Jack rejects the world of the "sheep" and the "herd" for the pure world of music for music's sake; and tries to use his French horn as the key to that world. Though he is good enough already to play for the Batavia Civic Orchestra, he will not play for his family. Someday they will "wake up and find him gone" (43). The horn becomes, as his mother observes, "his whole world" (44).

In making the horn his "whole world" and in rejecting the "herding warmth" (43) of his family as well as the community, Jack directly mirrors the language and life-style of Arcady Yegudkin, who appears here as in "Stillness." A splendid grotesque, Yegudkin speaks in similar fashion of the "idiot herds" outside his world of music. He is in fact as isolated from the community as Jack's father was, and as Jack wishes to be. Devoted to a single truth—music—Yegudkin is the personification of the self-absorbed and self-reflexive artist that Jack is in danger of becoming and that Gardner was at this time criticizing in the early chapters of *On Moral Fiction*. Jack has been consumed by a pride born of a desperately inflated sense of self. This false pride has corrupted him and separated him from his family, from his community, and from, by implication, his God. But Jack, as the title suggests, is redeemed, though in an ironic variation on the traditional epiphany, when Yegudkin tries out a new horn in Jack's presence. After an overwhelming display of musicianship, Yegudkin suddenly stops, yet the room continues to shimmer "like a vision." Without thinking, Jack asks Yegudkin if he will ever play that well. Yegudkin laughs loudly, his eyes widen, and he seems to grow "larger, beatific and demonic at once, like the music: overwhelming. 'Play like *me?*'" (47) he exclaims. Overwhelmed by the truth that he will never achieve this level of excellence, a truth underlined by Yegudkin's obvious astonishment, Jack now longs to be "far away safe" (47) from the world he had chosen in rejecting the world of guilt. Significantly, Jack hears no comment that day from Yegudkin (not entirely insensitive) about the "idiot herds," or the "stupidity of mankind." Both "beatific and demonic at once," Yegudkin has paradoxically saved him from the artistic self-absorption and isolation he has chosen. Returning home to the "herding warmth" of his family, Jack plunges into the crowd of "dazed-looking Saturday-morning shoppers herding along irritably, meekly, through the painfully bright light" (48).

When Gardner was asked, a few weeks before his death, why he wrote such a painful story, he replied:

> I had had a lot of trouble with my head: things like, I'm driving down the road, and I see this guilt scene, this old traumatic experience so vividly that I can't see the road, as hard as I try to concentrate, I can't break out of this vision. That's very dangerous: I had to hit the brakes and pray. That would happen to me quite often. So this guy said, "Write the story"; and when he said it, I could have killed him. How *terrifying* it was; such an immensely painful experience. And when you write a story, you have to see it over and over in your mind: copy down details, take out the ones that aren't important, and you finally get it. And it really did work . . . it's amazing. You actually do see your way through it. You keep staring at it and staring at it, and copying down like a scientist. . . . And when you're all done, you're OK. (Stanton 21)

Though Gardner implies that he was not "OK" before writing directly about his traumatic experience, he had written around his wound from the beginning of his career. It had kept him, as he puts it, "driven." And his initial attempts to confront the wound marked the first major steps forward in his apprenticeship as a writer. But to approach the wound directly was, he made clear, "immensely painful," a waking nightmare. As a defense, therefore, he did what Perseus and other reluctant heroes have always done: he used a shield to mirror the terrifying thing he felt compelled to face and overcome.

Initially, to mirror what he called his "guilt scene," Gardner created similarly ambiguous accidents involving characters radically different in appearance from him, even if psychologically true to one or more facets of his sensibility. Later, growing stronger emotionally, he stared at his "guilt scene" more directly, as in "Redemption."

David Cowart

Dark Night of the Soul

In all of the *King's Indian* stories Gardner describes victories—very small at first but finally substantial—over the darkness that forever threatens to swallow man's precarious enclaves of love, security, and order. He concedes the most to this darkness in the stories of "The Midnight Reader." The title of this section hints at the subject of each of the stories in it: someone's dark night of the soul. Yet each ends with some glimmer of light, manifested most commonly in a moment of renewal—of "resurrection," in Gardnerian parlance—for the main character. "Pastoral Care," perhaps the most cheerless story, explores a depressing number of spiritual dead ends, and the renewal of its protagonist, a priggish minister, comes at a terribly high cost. "The Ravages of Spring," on the other hand, offers literal resurrection through cloning. This story's darkness lies chiefly in its gothicism; though most of the tale takes place in the daytime, the reader experiences it as nocturnal, partly because of the greenish light of the ghastly weather in which the action transpires and partly because of the horrors revealed. The resurrection in "The Temptation of St. Ivo" is so understated as to pass easily unnoticed; it comes after the hero bravely hazards the spiritual credit of a lifetime of discipline. In "The Warden," set in dungeons and amid nocturnal burial parties, renewal merely flickers, a chimera or mockery. As one of the characters in a later story reflects, "It's always darkest before the dawn,"[1] and indeed the darkest of the stories in "The Midnight Reader" is this, the penultimate one. The last of this group, "John Napper Sailing Through the Universe," concerns a real-life painter, a friend of Gardner's, who wins an exemplary victory over despair. He wins it in his art, and this

Excerpted from *Arches and Light: The Fiction of John Gardner* by David Cowart (Carbondale: Southern Illinois University Press, 1983), 77–78; 99–100; 101; 109–110. © 1983 by the Board of Trustees, Southern Illinois University. Reprinted by permission of the publisher.

137

story heralds a spiritual and aesthetic dawn after the long night chron-
icled in "The Midnight Reader." . . .

Ship of State

Art's ability to remake the world, demonstrated in the Queen Louisa
stories, must be matched by an ability to probe truth in all its complexity. Gardner engages that complexity impressively in the short
novel that gives its title to the *King's Indian* collection. The author of
this "celebration of all literature and life" (p. 316) on occasion inti-
mated that he considered it one of his best works, and in multiplicity,
resonance, and sheer intellectual audacity it justifies his pride. The
narrator of "The King's Indian," Jonathan Upchurch, recalls his coming of age on an epic voyage of the whaler *Jerusalem*. Like the hero of
every initiation story, the nineteen-year-old Upchurch must take painful lessons in distinguishing the real from the ideal and the illusory. He
learns not only about the chicanery and duplicity of his fellow men but
also about the illusions built into existence itself. His tale, in fact, is
grounded in metaphysics; at sea in a craft he cannot pilot, he blithely
reflects: "In landlessness alone lies the highest truth, shoreless, as in-
definite as God!" (p. 212). This line, lifted almost verbatim from chapter 23 of *Moby Dick*, tells the reader that Upchurch's voyage will take
him away from security and stability (the land, in Melville's trope) into
the oceanic mystery of existence itself, for Melville describes the sea,
in the first chapter of his great novel, as an "image of the ungraspable
phantom of life." But along with metaphysics, the author of "The
King's Indian" takes an interest in ethics, politics, and aesthetics, and
the reader will discover corresponding symbolic dimensions to the
story. One recognizes in the *Jerusalem*, for example, the American ship
of state and in Jonathan Upchurch an artist-hero who addresses himself
to the complex relationship of truth and illusion in politics and art—
and explores once again the question of the artist's responsibility to
society. . . .

. . . The symbolism lends itself with greater consistency, however,
to something less grandiose—the voyage of the American ship of state.
Gardner's insistent, Whitmanesque capitalization of "Captain" ele-
vates the vessel's master to the status of founding father or president
(though surely not so credulous as Dirge, a number of the founding
fathers took seriously to the mumbo jumbo of Freemasonry). The first
idealistic dreamer, the archetypal Captain, charts a course extraordinary

in the annals of nations. His virtuous daughter—like Liberty aboard the American ship of state—will sail with him, defying the superstitious proscription of women at sea. But this first, inspired Captain is succeeded by less high-minded leaders: crass politicians, opportunists, and "bunkum artists" like Flint and Wilkins. The female passenger becomes a pasteboard ideal, if not something worse, and the great mission of the voyage comes more and more to be compromised. The crew must be fleshed out with slaves, and the rendezvous with destiny south of the Vanishing Isles begins to be forgotten as business—especially the larcenous "commerce" with other ships—proves increasingly lucrative. In this circumstance, the simultaneous allegiance to high principles and high profits, one finds the essential American paradox, the curious mixture of idealism and materialism that Fitzgerald captured in *The Great Gatsby*. But sooner or later, Gardner suggests, this dual vision must falter. The crew of the *Jerusalem*, many of whom once believed in their special destiny, become disenchanted as the adventure wears on and high expectations wane. . . .

. . . "The King's Indian" ends with Gardner's symbolic affirmation of the future of America. Even Miranda is redeemed. As the *Jerusalem's* lone female passenger, she has been seen as Liberty compromised, but in that the story turns on who shall possess her and for what ends, she can also be seen as a personification, like Hart Crane's Pocahontas, of the American Land. She is claimed at last by Jonathan, "monarch of Nowhere" (p. 242), who salutes her and his liberated, poly-racial crew in a voice significantly described as "orbiculate." This word would seem to mean simply that his tone is "rounded" or "orotund." But the word literally means "like a circle," and if one recalls that the circle symbolizes faith, one discovers a final comment of the Nowhere theme. Billy More, counseling Jonathan on survival in the rigging, tells him he can avoid the final step to Nowhere by keeping his mind on his faith. At the close, perched once again on "Nowhere's rim," Jonathan speaks in an "orbiculate" voice—a voice full of faith, and at that moment he embodies the extraordinary balancing act that has always characterized the American political ethos.

To a large extent faith is the subject of not only this tale but of the collection as a whole. Faith is the chief casualty of the dark night of the soul examined in "Pastoral Care" and the other stories of "The Midnight Reader." All of the characters in the first two sections of *The King's Indian* perch on the rim of despair, but some of them—John Napper, Queen Louisa—discover grounds for optimism about their condition. "The King's Indian" is a sunnier tale than its predecessors; it celebrates the nation that produced its author at the same time that it celebrates its own highspirited and redemptive art. But art figures directly or indirectly in nearly all of these stories. Those in which art figures least—"Pastoral Care" and "The Warden"—are also the bleakest, and those in which it is most central—"John Napper Sailing Through the Universe" and "The King's Indian"—are the brightest. Art, then, properly functions as an antidote to despair. The author of *The King's Indian*, not content merely to document the world's "bitter reality," fashions "new and wonderful possibilities," forges hope, keeps the faith.

Note

1. John Gardner, *The King's Indian: Stories and Tales* (New York: Knopf, 1974), p. 179. Hereafter cited parenthetically.

Geraldine DeLuca and Roni Natov

As John Gardner himself remarked recently in an interview, the critical response to his children's books has generally been respectful but unenthusiastic.[1] As a prolific scholar, critic, and novelist, he stirs some awe in reviewers, but no one seems to believe that his children's stories will appeal deeply to children. The children's literature journals have been fairly appreciative;[2] periodicals with a broader focus are a little impatient. For example, in *The Sewanee Review*, Bruce Allen writes: "Fanciful and clever as they are, the [fairy] tales remain ironic jokes which assert a breezy relativism. . . . My own children think the story ["The Shape-Shifters of Shorm"] makes no sense whatsoever. John Gardner might approve."[3]

Given his intrepidity as a writer and his concern with the loss of morality in art, it is not surprising that Gardner would try at some point to reach young readers. Moreover, with his interest in the medieval literary tradition and its moral, ironic, and leisurely modes of story telling, the fairy tale and the "collection" of stories would naturally appeal to him. And in fact all five children's works follow the tradition: three are fairy tale collections, one is a book of nonsense verse entitled *A Child's Bestiary*, and the last, *In the Suicide Mountains*, is a full-length work in the fairy tale mode. All are marked by Gardner's obvious talent and inventiveness, but all are partial failures. . . .

. . . Gardner's three small volumes of fairy tales, *Dragon, Dragon and Other Tales* (1975), *Gudgekin the Thistle Girl and Other Tales* (1976), and *The King of the Hummingbirds and Other Tales* (1977), are more substantial and reflect his interest in the form. Fairy tales clearly delineate what is good and what is evil, and Gardner is interested in the moral side of stories. He claims that literature should give us models of how to act and think, that fantasy, in particular, provides sunlight, where so much

Excerpted from "Modern Moralities for Children: John Gardner's Children's Books" by Geraldine DeLuca and Roni Natov, in *John Gardner: Critical Perspectives*, ed. Robert Morace and Kathryn Van Spanckeren (Carbondale: Southern Illinois University Press, 1982), 89–93. © 1982 by the Board of Trustees, Southern Illinois University. Reprinted by permission of the publisher.

modern realistic fiction for children is bleak and gloomy. He likes the simplicity of fairy tales and their focus on what is timeless and true. What he objects to is what he considers the oversimplified classist assumptions of traditional fairy tales, that there are good people and bad people, and that the good ones embody virtues espoused by the aristocracy. He claims that "solutions in my stories do not come about because of the wonderful power of the true-born aristocrat."[4] In his tales good characters can and often do perform evil deeds to survive; and cunning and necessity, which Gardner considers middle-class virtues, are highly valued.

It is not surprising, then, to find him applying modern novelistic techniques to the traditional fairy tale. The novel, having evolved as a middle-class form, serves Gardner in challenging traditional assumptions about heroism. His characters are not merely good or bad; they are depressed, bored, self-denying. As a novelist, he is interested in what inspires heroic impulses, what motivates destructive behavior. The result is a fusion of realism and fantasy. Gardner explores the extraordinariness of the ordinary the way Hans Christian Andersen did in his fairy tales, though Gardner rarely achieves the kind of emotional intensity or sympathy inspired by Andersen's stories or the power of Andersen's bite. Gardner's satirical touch is light; his tales are comic. Their peculiar blend of psychologizing and philosophizing with the plentiful details which specify and individualize characters and incidents creates much of their wit and humor. Gardner's Cinderella, Gudgekin the thistle girl, for example, needs to undergo a kind of psychotherapy with her fairy godmother before she achieves the right state of mind to accept her prince. In "The Shape-Shifters of Shorm," a tale about protean-like characters, the hero requests as his reward a "round-trip ticket to Brussels," and in the end, "changed his name to Zobrowski and dropped out of sight."[5] Gardner's particular mixture of the archetypal and the mundane reflects his personal vision of life: that the world often appears chaotic, that we don't really know what is going on, and therefore, that any action we decide upon may appear absurd and undermine a sense of meaning and order in the world. Like many contemporary writers, then, his sense of heroism is relative and reflects an essential uncertainty about ethics and codes of behavior.

At the center of many of Gardner's tales is a philosophical construct which reflects this concern with uncertainty. In one, a dragon ravages the countryside by tipping over fences, putting frogs in people's drinking water, tearing the last chapters out of novels, and changing house numbers around so that men crawl into bed with their neighbors' wives.[6] In another, a griffin, by his very presence, inspires such havoc that an experienced mason questions "which side of a brick is *up* and which side is *down*" and finds that because "the brick's top and bottom were impossible to tell apart . . . there was no way on earth he could be certain that the top was the top, and the bottom the bottom."[7] And in the last story of his most recent collection, a gnome changes shape so frequently that only in the end does he realize that the king, the billy goat, and the beautiful princess were none other than himself, and concludes: "'we've got to stop this fooling around and get back in touch.'"[8] Instead of evil, as in the traditional fairy tales, what is most threatening here is loss of control, memory, focus, essentially loss of touch with reality.

The chaos in the tales, of course, forces someone to figure out how order is to be restored. And according to Gardner, to cope with this chaotic and uncertain reality, we have developed "neat codes," rigid solutions, and defensive patterns. But these knightly codes with their traditional ingredients of wit and strength fail to work, as, for example, in "Dragon, Dragon." Gardner's characters can resolve the tales' problems and restore order only by abandoning their traditional, rigid behaviors and keeping their options open. Thus the solution to the king's problem in "The King of the Hummingbirds" comes not from the two eldest sons who fulfill the traditional expectations of heroes—that they embody intelligence and style—but from the youngest son's kindness. The hero in Gardner's stories is often a kind of simpleton who is least sure of what is ethical and proper. In fact, what makes the wise philosopher wise in "The Griffin and the Wise Old Philosopher" is his understanding of one of Gardner's favorite principles, the Heisenberg principle, which asserts that things are unknowable and reality uncertain. The philosopher tells his wife, "'I always start with the assumption that I know nothing, and probably nobody else knows much either.'"[9]

In addition to challenging the traditional assumptions that reality is knowable and that the world is or should be governed by the classical virtues of physical and intellectual excellence, Gardner wonders about what is true and good. He injects into the fairy tales a questioning of what is traditionally depicted as goodness: self-denial, martyrdom and sainthood. In "Gudgekin the Thistle Girl," Gudgekin never feels sorry for herself, only for others. She embraces her underdog position while her lot in life worsens. But her self-denial is followed by a bitter reversal: she becomes despairing and nihilistic. It is only when she learns to abandon her moral code, to enjoy the prince and her good fortune and to scorn martyrdom that she can be happy. In this tale Gardner not only warns against the dangers of self-renunciation, but he insists that self-degradation can lead to the insatiable cruelty of Gudgekin's step-mother whose "fear of humiliation so drove her that she was never satisfied."[10] He also demonstrates in "The Tailor and the Giant" how the little tailor's self-preserving impulse not only releases him from impotence and cowardice, but frees the armies of gallant young men from the giant's prison.

Gardner clearly asserts an appropriately modern psychological view—self-worth is good; self-denial is harmful. But he is also aware of how often, when confronted with the question of whether someone is trustworthy or destructive, "a person just can't tell."[11] How much of this philosophizing and psychologizing comes through to children is questionable. Gardner claims that his tales are meant for older kids "who have been through fairy tales and are ready for slight variety."[12] It would seem that he's referring to precocious grade-schoolers and adolescents. But the sophisticated humor and psychological insights of his most successful stories suggest that they might really fare best with adults.

Notes

1. See Roni Natov and Geraldine DeLuca, "An Interview with John Gardner," *The Lion and the Unicorn*, 2 (Spring 1978), 129.

2. See, for example, *The Horn Book*, 54 (April 1978), 194–95, and *Language Arts*, 54 (March 1977), 330.

3. Bruce Allen, "Settling for Ithaca: The Fictions of John Gardner," *The Sewanee Review*, 85 (July 1977), 528.

4. Natov and DeLuca, p. 118.

5. "The Shape-Shifters of Shorm," in *Gudgekin the Thistle Girl and Other Tales* (New York: Knopf, 1976), p. 52.

6. From "Dragon, Dragon," in *Dragon, Dragon and Other Tales* (New York: Knopf, 1975).

7. "The Griffin and the Wise Old Philosopher," in *Gudgekin the Thistle Girl and Other Tales*, pp. 24–25.

8. "The Gnome and the Dragon," in *The King of the Hummingbirds and Other Tales* (New York: Knopf, 1977), p. 58.

9. In *Gudgekin the Thistle Girl and Other Tales*, p. 31.

10. *Gudgekin*, p. 8.

11. From "The Miller's Mule," in *Dragon, Dragon and Other Tales*, p. 54.

12. Natov and DeLuca, p. 119.

David Cowart

The longest fiction in *The Art of Living*, "Vlemk the Box-Painter" runs to novella length, but unlike the title novella in *The King's Indian*, it neither concludes nor gives its name to the volume. Gardner's diffidence on this point might suggest that he hesitated to claim as much for this story as for its counterpart in the earlier collection; on the other hand he did not publish "The King's Indian" separately, and he did "Vlemk." The story that can most profitably be compared with "Vlemk," however, is another from the earlier collection: "John Napper Sailing Through the Universe." Both concern an artist who attempts faithfully to reproduce physical reality, only to find himself "gazing . . . into the abyss" (p. 170). But one would err to dismiss "Vlemk" as "John Napper" warmed over. Gardner evidently felt the need to treat the subject of the artist's emotional and psychological health at greater length that he had done earlier. The extra length also enables him to explore more fully the effects of the protagonist's art on the social milieu. One notes too, that the mode of realistic memoir in which "John Napper" is written gives way to the mode of fable or parable in "Vlemk." Thus Gardner makes the same transition his artists make—from realism to fantasy, or rather from reality to the inner vision that transforms reality.

One may wonder why Gardner gives his hero such an odd profession. Why a box-painter? Vlemk's boxes—people buy them as presents—may never actually contain anything. A painter of vacuity, he produces art that would seem to exemplify Oscar Wilde's dictum that all art is essentially useless. But one may argue that art counters the "comic futility" (p. 150) of the universe. In such a futile universe (Italo Calvino, a favorite of Gardner's, would call it "cosmicomic"), man exists in a perennial predicament, a permanent fix. To be in this kind of trouble is to be, in Vlemk's own favorite phrase, "in a box" existen-

Excerpted from *Arches and Light: The Fiction of John Gardner* by David Cowart (Carbondale: Southern Illinois University Press, 1983), 179–82. © 1983 by the Board of Trustees, Southern Illinois University. Reprinted by permission of the publisher.

145

tially. Art exists to decorate this box, and Vlemk is thus the archetypal artist.

The portrait of the princess that is at once Vlemk's glory and his folly is the proverbial "speaking likeness" made literal. That the picture's first words take away Vlemk's powers of speech reminds the reader of another commonplace: an artist's work does his talking for him. When Vlemk falls mute, one understands that a painter who records reality so slavishly has, in effect, nothing of his own to say. He regains the ability to speak when he improves the portrait according to the dictates of a personal vision. The picture's continuing to talk after its alteration argues that Vlemk still has departed not a whit from reality. But now the reality is the one he has created.

He has also created himself, for his intimacy with the painting, the fact that they are always together until he takes it to the woman he loves, suggests a psychological component, a projection of the anima with which he must come to terms as part of his psychological maturation. But the anima exists in a variety of forms, and Vlemk also projects her in his flattering portrait of the barmaid. "He'd lifted her breasts a little, tightened her skin, raised a sagging eyebrow, increased the visibility of her dimple. In short, he'd made her beautiful, and he'd done it so cunningly that no one but an artist could have told you where the truth left off and the falsehood began." The point here is that the portrait lies only temporarily, because the barmaid grows "increasingly similar to the fraudulent painting, smiling as she served her customers, looking at strangers with the eyes of an innocent, standing so erect, in her foolish pride, that her breasts were almost exactly where Vlemk had painted them" (p. 161). She has been transformed by a painting. She goes from harridan to cheerful pinup, and by the end of the story she has graduated from prostitute to married woman.

In painting the princess, Vlemk does exactly the opposite of what he does in painting the barmaid. The barmaid sees an ideal and grows into it, her sagging eyebrow rising to the level of the painted one; the princess sees the truth about herself and despairs, so that the drooping eyelid of a painted likeness merely accelerates the decline of its counterpart in the living face. In various paintings of the princess Vlemk promotes her every velleity to the status of confirmed character trait. Miserably, the princess fulfills every painted prophecy: "The Princess Looking Bored," "The Princess Considers Revenge," "The Dream of Debauchery," "The Princess Gives Way to Wrath," and so forth.

The unhappy princess and the king her father enable Gardner to realize the theme of art's effect on society with great economy. As Vlemk proceeds through the stages of his artistic development—meticulous craftsman, unsparing naturalist, despondent dauber, soulless calendar realist—the princess registers the effects. Her moral and physical health seems related in an almost magical way to Vlemk's art, for she reacts to it even when she has not seen it. When he is just a good painter, at the beginning, she is lovely but rather heartless; after his unsparing portrait of her, followed by the terrible "Reality boxes" (p. 172), he visits her and wonders at her incipient physical decline. At this time the reader learns of her father the king's mysterious malady. The king, visibly dying, fears that his daughter will fall victim to the disease that wastes him, and he intuits the existence of a curse somehow associated with Vlemk. "Beg him to remove the curse," pleads the king. "Otherwise we're doomed" (p. 200). The curse, of which Vlemk remains ignorant, is the curse of bad art. But if the sickness in the royal family and in the kingdom for which it stands stems from the failure of Vlemk and his fellow artists to do their duty, the society deserves part of the blame for failing to honor its artists properly. The trio of embittered or impotent artists at the tavern—ex-poet, ex-violinist, would-be axe-murderer—illustrates the status of the artist in this society, which honors only artisans like the bell caster, the gargoyle carver, and the stained-glass-window maker. The story's hero, the only real artist who practices, falls slave to a flawed and deadly aesthetic which eats away at the society symbolically in the persons of its monarch and his daughter. Once he fights his way free of that debilitating aesthetic, Vlemk lifts the curse on the royal family and the curse on himself. When he marries the princess, now queen, insuring the prestige of at least one artist, he completes the undoing of the vicious circle in which bad art, despised artists, and a sick society feed on each other.

Gregory L. Morris

For the narrator of "The Library Horror," . . . art comes terrifyingly close to life, as literary characters fill his library and craze his imagination. Winfred, the protagonist, is a bookish man from "a family of lunatics" (p. 88). He sits one night worrying over Susanne Langer's *Problems of Art*, with its idea of virtual space, or "space that seems as real as any other until the moment you try to enter it, at which time it proves an apparition" (p. 90). Langer argues that artistic creations have a life or "living form" of their own; a literary character, "though it is a created apparition, a pure appearance, is objective; it seems to be charged with feeling because its form expresses the very nature of feeling. Therefore, it is an *objectification* of subjective life, and so is every other work of art."[1] Art has a virtual existence, an "autonomous life."

This, in fact, is what Winfred discovers when he explores the noises that have been coming for the last few days from behind his library door. Penknife in hand, he opens the door and enters the tomblike room. . . . In Winfred's library stand Raskolnikov and a woman who might be Becky Sharp, both moral outcasts, but she an outcast "from a morality so different from his own world's as to cast the idea of 'universal human nature' into the trash-heap of ancient *pseudodoxia*" (p. 93). They disappear "into the dimness beyond the fourth shelf," worlds and times apart yet similar enough in temperament to go off together as, perhaps, lovers.

The reality of Winfred's vision is the obvious question. Winfred's wife stands outside the door, telling him it is time to go to bed, concerned for his welfare within the library walls. And well might she be concerned, for as her words melt into air a new vision, a new apparition comes rushing from the bookshelf toward Winfred, "brighter than the light from a bursting star, coming straight at me with a clatter and a roar like a lightning-ball" (p. 94). It is Achilles, "the hero of absolute

Excerpted from *A World of Order and Light: The Fiction of John Gardner* by Gregory L. Morris (Athens: University of Georgia Press, 1984), 193–95. © 1984 by the University of Georgia Press. Reprinted by permission.

justice, God-sent doom, terrible purgation" (p. 95). Achilles waves his huge sword over Winfred's head, hesitates for a moment at the sound of a woman's voice from beyond the door, then slices downward into Winfred's shoulder: "Not to make too much of it, I knew then and there that I was dying" (p. 95).

An interesting question: is Winfred *actually* or *virtually* dying? Are the characters so real, is Achilles' sword so sharp and so cold that it truly cuts Winfred's flesh? Winfred thinks so, the blood and life running out of him. But perhaps he is just crazy, another lunatic in a long line of lunatics? Even Winfred considers this possibility: "Here sits character *x*, a madman, struck a mortal blow by character *y*, a fiction. What can *x* do, mad as he is, but struggle to maintain justice, normality?" (p. 96). Winfred begins to think of himself as a character in a fiction—which he is. And he also begins to construct a fiction of his own, in an attempt to right a possible injustice and to give immortality to his wife and to his father: "If a fictional character, namely Achilles, can make blood run down my chest (if it is indeed running down my chest), then a living character, or two such characters—my father and my wife—can be made to live forever, simply by being put in a fiction" (p. 96). The loverlike combination of father and daughter-in-law is akin to the coupling of Raskolnikov with the Becky Sharp figure: "He's eighty-two. She's thirty. No one would think him insane except that he once backed his truck through the plate-glass window of my bank" (p. 99). Fiction becomes a convenient means to immortality.

Even Winfred looks for convenience at the end, as the desk fills with blood and his head fills with "planets and stars": "'Dear Heavenly Father,' I whisper with all my might, for any good fiction will serve in hard times—I clench my eyes against the tumbling of the planets—'Dear Heavenly Father,' I whisper with all my might" (p. 100). Winfred's prayer trails off into silence, the story ending without punctuation, without proper finish. It is left incomplete by Gardner, who creates Winfred as a character in his own fiction and who believes, with Langer, that art has a virtual existence of its own. That is part of Gardner's aesthetic, that art is the objectification of subjective feeling. Such things *could* happen.

Toward the end of his story, Winfred begs of Achilles, "No justice . . . enough of justice!" Winfred has had enough of the cold-handed, clear-eyed justice of the gods and the godlike. Justice among the divine and the fictional is much easier than among the human here on earth.

Note

1. Susanne K. Langer, *Problems of Art* (New York: Charles Scribner's Sons, 1957), p. 9. Gardner, in response to a question about the generation of ideas for his fiction, once remarked in an interview: "Just recently I was reading a book on aesthetics, which I had heard about for a long time, and I found it very exciting and got three short stories out of it." See Ed Christian, "An Interview with John Gardner," *Prairie Schooner* 54 (Winter 1980–81): 82–83.

Chronology

For many details of Gardner's life through 1979 I am indebted to the chronology worked out by John Howell and published in his *John Gardner: A Bibliographical Profile*. I am also indebted to Howell for some additional information not included there.

1933   John Champlin Gardner, Jr., born 21 July, eldest of four children of John Champlin and Priscilla Jones Gardner, Batavia, New York.

1945   Death, on 4 April, of brother Gilbert, run over by a cultipacker (a heavy farm implement) Gardner was pulling behind a tractor.

1948   First "professional" publication: a cartoon of an elephant, published in July issue of *Seventeen Magazine*.

1951   Graduates from Batavia High School; enters DePauw University, intending to major in chemistry.

1951–1955   Publishes a story ("Freshman") in the 15 February 1951 issue of *Boulder*, a campus magazine at DePauw. Marries Joan Louise Patterson on 6 June 1953 and transfers to Washington University in St. Louis. Literary and philosophical interests develop; under the influence of a respected teacher, Jarvis Thurston (editor of *Perspective*), begins writing material later incorporated into *Nickel Mountain*. In senior year elected to Phi Beta Kappa and wins Woodrow Wilson fellowship.

1955–1958   Enters creative writing program at the University of Iowa. Receives M.A. for a creative thesis comprising four short stories ("Darkling Wood," "One Saturday Morning," "Peter Willis, Resting," and "Nickel Mountain"). In 1955, short story "Nickel Mountain" published in *Reflections: Washington University Student Review*. Pursues academic study in medieval language and literature. Earns Ph.D. in 1958 with a creative dissertation, the unpublished novel "The Old Men"; completes another novel, "Sparrows," also unpublished.

1958   Appointed to lectureship at Oberlin College; fired in the same year for (according to Gardner) leading a faculty strike.

1959–1962   Accepts lectureship at Chico State College (now California State University at Chico); teaches creative writing and supervises student literary magazine. Birth of son, Joel, 31 December 1959. Begins professional literary magazine, *MSS*, which in its three numbers (1961, 1962, 1964) publishes material by Joyce Carol Oates, William Gass, John Hawkes, Howard Nemerov, George P. Elliot, William Stafford, William Palmer, W. S. Merwin, and others. In 1961, "A Little Night Music" published in *Northwest Review*. Birth of daughter, Lucy, 3 January 1962. In collaboration with a colleague, Lennis Dunlap, publishes first book, *The Forms of Fiction* (1962).

1962–1965   Accepts assistant professorship at San Francisco State College (now called San Francisco State University) to teach medieval studies. Translates *The Alliterative Morte Arthure* and *The Complete Works of the Gawain-Poet* and writes a lengthy study of the life and works of Chaucer. In 1963, "The Edge of the Woods" published in *Quarterly Review of Literature*. Has completed *The Resurrection* and a version of *Nickel Mountain*. In March 1965, New American Library accepts *The Resurrection* for publication and shows interest in *Nickel Mountain*; Gardner begins work on *The Sunlight Dialogues*. *The Complete Works of the Gawain-Poet* published 31 August 1965.

1965–1969   Begins appointment in September 1965 as associate professor of English (to teach Old English and medieval studies) at Southern Illinois University in Carbondale. Buys farm with large old house on Boskydell Road, south of Carbondale. Continues work on *The Sunlight Dialogues* and writes early draft of *On Moral Fiction*. In 1966 "Nickel Mountain" published in *Southern Review*. Gardner's first published novel, *The Resurrection*, published 22 June 1966. "The Spike in the Door" published in *Ball State*

University Forum in 1967. By August 1969, completes *The Wreckage of Agathon* and begins work on *Grendel*.

1970 By March, has completed, in collaboration with his wife, Joan, *The Smugglers of Lost Souls' Rock* (the "inner" novel in *October Light*). By June, has completed *Grendel*. In summer, in York, England, begins epic poem *Jason and Medeia*. By fall, has won a Danforth fellowship and is distinguished visiting professor at the University of Detroit. *The Wreckage of Agathon* published by Harper & Row. Knopf buys *Grendel* and *The Sunlight Dialogues*.

1971 "The Grave" published in *Quarterly Review of Literature*. Writes most of the stories later published in *The King's Indian*. In September, *Grendel* is published, as is *The Alliterative Morte Arthure*. By this time Gardner is on sabbatical in London, working on *Jason and Medeia* and other projects.

1972 Completes draft of *Jason and Medeia*; begins revision of *Nickel Mountain*. Receives a grant from the National Endowment for the Arts. Achieves popular fame as a novelist with publication in December of best-selling *The Sunlight Dialogues*. Also publishes "The Darkening Green" in *Iowa Review*; "The Thing[s]," in *Perspective*; "Pastoral Care," in *Audience*; and an excerpt from "The Temptation of St. Ivo," in *Esquire*.

1973 Gardner is visiting professor at Northwestern University for the winter quarter. Is awarded a Guggenheim fellowship. "The Ravages of Spring" published in *Fantastic Science Fiction and Fantasy Stories*. *Jason and Medeia* published in June, *Nickel Mountain* in December, both by Knopf.

1974 "The Music Lover" published, in *Antaeus: Special Fiction Issue*; "King Gregor and the Fool" published, in *Atlantic Monthly*; "The Joy of the Just" published, in *American Poetry Review*. In August, Gardner teaches at the Bread Loaf Writers' Conference; *The Construction of the Wakefield Cycle* published. From 8 September to 5 October, Gardner tours Japan for the U.S. Information Service. "John Napper Sailing through the Universe" published, in *Modern Occasions 2 New Fiction, Criticism, Poetry*. "The Things" re-

153

printed in *Prize Stories 1974: The O. Henry Awards.* "The Warden" published, in *Tri-Quarterly.* Gardner accepts a Hadley Fellowship appointment at Bennington College for 1974–1975. Begins work on *Shadows*; works on children's stories. *The King's Indian: Stories and Tales* published in December.

1975   Buys a house in Old Bennington, Vermont; begins work on *October Light. The Construction of Christian Poetry in Old English* published. Gardner elected to membership in the American Academy of Arts and Letters. Works on various radio plays for National Public Radio. Teaches again at Bread Loaf. "Queen Louisa" reprinted in *Superfiction, or The American Story Transformed: An Anthology.*

1976   Finishes work on *October Light* and *In the Suicide Mountains*; works on *On Moral Fiction.* Resigns professorship at Southern Illinois University. Leaves his wife, Joan, and moves to Cambridge, New York. "King of the Hummingbirds" published in the *Saturday Evening Post* (April); "The Pear Tree" published in the *Saturday Evening Post* (October); "Trumpeter" published in *Esquire* (December); *October Light*, Gardner's third best-selling novel (along with *The Sunlight Dialogues* and *Nickel Mountain*), published in December.

1977   *October Light* wins the National Book Critics Circle Award for Fiction in 1976. *Rumpelstiltskin*, one of three operas for which Gardner wrote the librettos, is produced. *The Poetry of Chaucer* (Southern Illinois University Press) and *The Life and Times of Chaucer* (Knopf) published. "Redemption" published in *Atlantic Monthly* (May). Lectures on American literature at Salzburg, Austria. Teaches again at Bread Loaf. Accepts a position as writer in residence at George Mason University. *A Child's Bestiary* and *In the Suicide Mountains* published. In December, enters Johns Hopkins Hospital for (successful) cancer surgery.

1978   "Stillness" published in *Hudson Review* (Winter 1977–78); "Redemption" reprinted in *The Best American Short Stories 1978. On Moral Fiction* published by Basic Books. Teaches at Bread Loaf. Joins English faculty at the State University of New York at Binghamton, where he remains as director of the creative writing program until his death. *Poems* published by the Lord John Press. *Rumpelstiltskin* published by New London Press.

1979 Operas *Frankenstein* and *William Wilson* published by New London Press. "The Library Horror" published, in *Seattle Review* (Spring 1979). "Nimram" published, in *Atlantic Monthly* (September 1979). *Vlemk the Box-Painter* published by Lord John Press.

1980 *Freddy's Book* published. On 17 February, marries poet L. M. (Liz) Rosenberg, a few days after divorce from first wife, Joan.

1981 *The Art of Living and Other Stories* published. *MSS: A Retrospective* published.

1982 *Mickelsson's Ghosts*, Gardner's largest novel since *The Sunlight Dialogues*, published; although he hopes *Mickelsson's Ghosts* will repair the damage his reputation suffered as a result of the controversy surrounding *On Moral Fiction*, reviews are disappointing. On 8 September, is divorced from Liz Rosenberg. On 14 September, dies in an accident near his home in Susquehanna, Pennsylvania, as a result of losing control of his motorcycle, a few days before his intended marriage to Susan Thornton.

1983 *On Becoming a Novelist* published by Harper & Row.

1984 *The Art of Fiction* published by Knopf. Translation of ancient Mesopotamian epic *Gilgamesh* published by Knopf. "Julius Caesar and the Werewolf" published in *Playboy* (September).

1986 *Stillness* (an intensely autobiographical account of Gardner's life with his first wife, Joan) and *Shadows* (an unfinished novel) published by Knopf, edited and introduced by Nicholas Delbanco.

Selected Bibliography

Primary Works

Manuscript Collection

The John Gardner Collection. Papers. The University of Rochester Library, Department of Rare Books and Special Collections, Rochester, New York.

Short Fiction Collections

The Art of Living and Other Stories. New York: Knopf, 1981. Includes "Nimram," "Redemption," "Stillness," "The Music Lover," "Trumpeter," "The Library Horror," "The Joy of the Just," "Vlemk the Box-Painter," "Come on Back" (all previously published), and "The Art of Living."

Dragon, Dragon and Other Tales. New York: Knopf, 1975. Includes "Dragon, Dragon," "The Tailor and the Giant," "The Miller's Mule," and "The Last Piece of Light."

Gudgekin the Thistle Girl and Other Tales. New York: Knopf, 1976. Includes "Gudgekin the Thistle Girl," "The Griffin and the Wise Old Philosopher," "The Shape-Shifters of Shorm," and "The Sea Gulls."

The King of the Hummingbirds and Other Tales. New York: Knopf, 1977. Includes "The King of the Hummingbirds" (previously published), "The Witch's Wish," "The Pear Tree" (previously published), and "The Gnome and the Dragon."

The King's Indian: Stories and Tales. New York: Knopf, 1974. Includes "Pastoral Care," "The Ravages of Spring," "The Temptation of St. Ivo," "The Warden," "John Napper Sailing through the Universe" (all previously published), "Queen Louisa," "King Gregor and the Fool" (previously published), "Muriel," and "The King's Indian."

Uncollected Short Fiction

"The Darkening Green." *Iowa Review* 3 (Winter 1972): 46–48.

"The Edge of the Woods." *Quarterly Review of Literature* 11, no. 3 (1963): 268–301. Revised for *Nickel Mountain*.

"Freshman." *Boulder* [DePauw] 15 (February 1952): 1, 20.

"The Grave." *Quarterly Review of Literature* 17, no. 3–4 (1971): 354–71. Revised for *Nickel Mountain.*
"Julius Caesar and the Werewolf." *Playboy,* (September 1984), 74–78, 86, 174–80. Posthumous.
"A Little Night Music." *Northwest Review* 4 (Spring 1961): 30–40. Revised for *The Sunlight Dialogues.*
"Nickel Mountain." *Reflections: Washington University Student Review* 4 (1955): 42–56.
"Nickel Mountain." *Southern Review,* n.s. 1 (Spring 1966): 374–418. Revision and expansion of previous entry. Revised for *Nickel Mountain.*
"The Spike in the Door." *Ball State University Forum* 8 (Autumn 1967): 52–55.
"The Thing[s]." *Perspective* 17 (Winter 1972): 17–27. Letter *s* inadvertently omitted from title. Revised for *Nickel Mountain.*

Works in Other Literary Genres

A Child's Bestiary. New York: Knopf, 1977. Children's poetry.
Death and the Maiden. Dallas: New London Press, 1979. Play.
Frankenstein. Dallas: New London Press, 1979. Libretto.
Freddy's Book. New York: Knopf, 1980. Novel.
Grendel. New York: Knopf, 1971. Novel.
In the Suicide Mountains. New York: Knopf, 1977. Children's novel.
Jason and Medeia. New York: Knopf, 1973. Epic poem.
Mickelsson's Ghosts. New York: Knopf, 1982. Novel.
Nickel Mountain. New York: Knopf, 1973. Novel.
October Light. New York: Knopf, 1976. Novel.
Poems. Northridge, CA: Lord John Press, 1978.
The Resurrection. New York: New American Library, 1966. Novel.
Rumpelstiltskin. Dallas: New London Press, 1978. Libretto.
Stillness and Shadows. Ed. Nicholas Delbanco. New York: Knopf, 1986. Novels. Posthumous.
The Sunlight Dialogues. New York: Knopf, 1972. Novel.
The Temptation Game. Dallas: New London Press, 1980. Play.
William Wilson. Dallas: New London Press, 1979. Libretto.
The Wreckage of Agathon. New York: Harper, 1970. Novel.

Criticism and Translations

The Alliterative Morte Arthure. Carbondale: Southern Illinois University Press, 1971.
The Art of Fiction. New York, Knopf, 1984. Posthumous.
The Complete Works of the Gawain-Poet. Chicago: University of Chicago Press, 1965.

The Construction of Christian Poetry in Old English. Carbondale: Southern Illinois University Press, 1975.

The Construction of the Wakefield Cycle. Carbondale: Southern Illinois University Press, 1974.

With Lennis Dunlap. *The Forms of Fiction.* New York: Random, 1962.

With John Maier. *Gilgamesh.* New York: Knopf, 1984. Posthumous.

The Life and Times of Chaucer. New York: Knopf, 1977.

On Becoming a Novelist. New York: Harper, 1983. Posthumous.

On Moral Fiction. New York: Basic Books, 1978.

The Poetry of Chaucer. Carbondale: Southern Illinois University Press, 1977.

With Nobuko Tsukui. *Tengu Child: Stories by Kikuo Itaya.* Carbondale: Southern Illinois University Press, 1983. Posthumous.

Secondary Works

Interviews

Bellamy, Joe David, and Pat Ensworth. "John Gardner." In *The New Fiction: Interviews with Innovative American Writers,* edited by Joe David Bellamy, 169–93. Urbana: University of Illinois Press, 1974.

Christian, Ed. "An Interview with John Gardner." *Prairie Schooner* 54 (Winter 1980): 70–93.

Harkness, James. "Interview: John Gardner." *News* (SUNY), April 1979, Forum section, 1–2, 7–8.

Harvey, Marshall L. "Where Philosophy and Fiction Meet: An Interview with John Gardner." *Chicago Review* 29, no. 4 (1978): 73–87.

Laskin, Daniel. "Challenging the Literary Naysayers." *Horizon* 21 (July 1978): 32–36.

Natov, Roni, and Geraldine DeLuca. "An Interview with John Gardner." *The Lion and the Unicorn: A Journal of Children's Literature* 2, no. 1 (Spring 1978): 114–36.

Stanton, Davis M. "The Last Interview of John Gardner." *Croton Review* 6 (1983): 1, 20–21.

Books and Parts of Books

Carver, Raymond. Foreword to *On Becoming a Novelist,* by John Gardner, xi–xix. New York: Harper, 1983.

Cowart, David. *Arches and Light: The Fiction of John Gardner.* Carbondale: Southern Illinois University Press, 1983.

DeLuca, Geraldine, and Roni Natov. "Modern Moralities for Children: John Gardner's Children's Books." In *John Gardner: Critical Perspectives,* edited by Robert A. Morace and Kathryn Van Spanckeren, 89–96. Carbondale: Southern Illinois University Press, 1982.

Greiner, Donald J. "Sailing through *The King's Indian* with John Gardner and His Friends." In *John Gardner: Critical Perspectives*, edited by Robert A. Morace and Kathryn Van Spanckeren, 76–88. Carbondale: Southern Illinois University Press, 1982.

Henderson, Jeff, ed. *Thor's Hammer: Essays on John Gardner.* Conway: University of Central Arkansas Press, 1985.

Howell, John M. "The Wound and the Albatross: John Gardner's Apprenticeship." In *Thor's Hammer: Essays on John Gardner*, edited by Jeff Henderson, 1–16. Conway: University of Central Arkansas Press, 1985.

Johnson, Charles. *The Sorcerer's Apprentice: Tales and Conjurations.* New York: Atheneum, 1986.

Morace, Robert A., and Kathryn Van Spanckeren, eds. *John Gardner: Critical Perspectives.* Carbondale: Southern Illinois University Press, 1982.

Morris, Gregory L. *A World of Order and Light: The Fiction of John Gardner.* Athens: University of Georgia Press, 1984.

Neilson, Keith. Commentary on *The King's Indian: Stories and Tales*, by John Gardner. In *Masterplots Annual 1975*, edited by Frank N. Magill, 164–66. Englewood Cliffs, N.J.: Salem Press, 1976.

Payne, Alison R. "Clown, Monster, Magician: The Purpose of Lunacy in John Gardner's Fiction." In *Thor's Hammer: Essays on John Gardner*, edited by Jeff Henderson, 157–66. Conway: University of Central Arkansas Press, 1985.

Roberts, Millard F. *A Narrative History of Remsen, New York.* Syracuse: Author, 1914.

Wegner, Hart. "'Dear Hart, Dear Heorot': John Gardner as Editor." In *Thor's Hammer: Essays on John Gardner*, edited by Jeff Henderson, 75–88. Conway: University of Central Arkansas Press, 1985.

Journal Articles and Reviews

Allen, Bruce. "Settling for Ithaca: The Fictions of John Gardner." *Sewanee Review* 85 (Summer 1977): 520–31.

———. "From Gardner, Short Stories Dimmed by Abstractions." Review of *The Art of Living and Other Stories*, by John Gardner. *Christian Science Monitor*, 24 June 1981, 17.

Coale, Sam. "Oddball Insights in 'Art of Living,'" Review of *The Art of Living and Other Stories*, by John Gardner. *Providence Journal*, 31 May 1981, np.

Cockshutt, Rod. "Gardner Needs to Lie Fallow." Review of *The King's Indian: Stories and Tales*, by John Gardner. *Raleigh News and Observer*, 2 February 1975, n. pag.

Derrickson, Howard. "Dazzling Tales from Gardner." Review of *The King's*

Indian: Stories and Tales, by John Gardner. *St. Louis Globe-Democrat*, 4–5 January 1975, D4.

Friedman, Alan. "A John Gardner Spectrum, from Gothic Horrors to Romantic Realism." Review of *The King's Indian: Stories and Tales*, by John Gardner. *New York Times Book Review*, 15 December 1974, 1–2.

Fuller, Edmund. "Box Painter, Ax Murderer, Imperial Dog." Review of *The Art of Living and Other Stories*, by John Gardner. *Wall Street Journal*, 29 June 1981, 20.

Garfitt, Roger. "Fiction and Fabulation." Review of *The King's Indian: Stories and Tales*, by John Gardner. *Times Literary Supplement*, 12 December 1975, 1477.

Gelfant, Blanche H. "Fiction Chronicle." Review of *The King's Indian: Stories and Tales*, by John Gardner. *Hudson Review* 28 (Summer 1975): 309–11.

Harris, Roger. "Gardner Lifts the Short Story to New Heights." *Newark* (N.J.) *Star Ledger*, n.d., April 1981, n.pag.

Henderson, Jeff. "John Gardner's *Jason and Medeia:* The Resurrection of a Genre." *Papers on Language and Literature* 22, no. 1 (Winter 1986): 76–95.

Le Guin, Ursula. "Where Giants Roam." Review of *Freddy's Book* and *Vlemk the Box-Painter*, by John Gardner. *Washington Post Book World*, 23 March 1980, 1, 5.

Moody, Minnie Hite. "You May Not Dig, but Still Read On." Review of *The King's Indian: Stories and Tales*, by John Gardner. *Columbus Evening Dispatch*, 26 January 1975, sec. 1, 6.

Moynahan, Julian. "Moral Fictions." Review of *The Art of Living and Other Stories*, by John Gardner. *New York Times Book Review*, 17 May 1981, 7, 27–28.

Murray, James G. Review of *The King's Indian: Stories and Tales*, by John Gardner. *Critic* 33 (March 1975): 71–73.

Parrill, William. "Words and Pictures in Closest Harmony." Review of *The King's Indian: Stories and Tales*, by John Gardner. *Nashville Tennessean*, 12 January 1975, F6.

Thompson, Francis J. "Hedge against Inflation." Review of *The King's Indian: Stories and Tales*, by John Gardner. *Tampa Tribune-Times*, 26 January 1975, C5.

Tyler, Anne. "Little Miracles: In Gardner's Fine Stories, Questions in the Stillness." Review of *The Art of Living and Other Stories*, by John Gardner. *Detroit News*, 10 May 1981, J2.

Bibliographies

Howell, John M. *John Gardner: A Bibliographical Profile*. Carbondale: Southern Illinois University Press, 1980.

Morace, Robert A. *John Gardner: An Annotated Secondary Bibliography*. New York: Garland, 1984.

Index

The Author

Jeff Henderson is a professor of English at the University of Central Arkansas in Conway, Arkansas, and acquisitions editor of the UCA Press. He received his B.A. in English from the University of Central Arkansas in 1963, his M.A. in English from Southern Illinois University–Carbondale in 1965, and his Ph.D. in English (medieval language and literature) in 1971 from Southern Illinois University, where John Gardner was his dissertation director. He currently serves on the editorial boards of *Publications of the Arkansas Philological Association*, *Slant: A Journal of Poetry*, and *American Journalism*. His publications on John Gardner include essays in *American Literature*, *Papers on Language and Literature*, and *Thor's Hammer: Essays on John Gardner*, of which he was editor, and reviews in *PAPA*, *American Literature*, and *South Atlantic Review*. He has also published articles on Chaucer, Thomas Hardy, G. M. Hopkins, the state of literacy in present-day America, and other topics. For four and a half years he wrote a weekly newspaper column, "Toad Suck Country," that was primarily concerned with the metaphysical implications of bass fishing.

The Editor

Gorden Weaver earned his Ph.D. in English and creative writing at the University of Denver, and is currently professor of English at Oklahoma State University. He is the author of several novels, including *Count a Lonely Cadence, Give Him a Stone, Circling Byzantium,* and *The Eight Corners of the World,* and his short stories are collected in *The Entombed Man of Thule, Such Waltzing Was Not Easy, Getting Serious, Morality Play,* and *A World Quite Round.* Recognition of his fiction includes the St. Lawrence Award for Fiction, two National Endowment for the Arts fellowships and the O. Henry First Prize. He edited *The American Short Story, 1945–1980: A Critical History* and is currently editor of the *Cimarron Review.* Married, and the father of three daughters, he lives in Stillwater, Oklahoma.